NEVER GIVE UP

Written by Jan Owens

Copyright © 2008 by Jan Owens

NEVER GIVE UP
by Jan Owens

Printed in the United States of America

ISBN 978-1-60647-876-9

All rights reserved solely by the author. The author guarantees all contents are original and do not infringe upon the legal rights of any other person or work. No part of this book may be reproduced in any form without the permission of the author. The views expressed in this book are not necessarily those of the publisher.

Unless otherwise indicated, Bible quotations are taken from King James Version of the Bible. Notated references are from the Amplified Version, Copyright © 1965, by Zondervan Publishing House.

www.xulonpress.com

Dedication

This book is dedicated with all my love to my children and grandchildren which includes my precious sons-in-law and daughter-in-law: Steve and Charlene, Lori and Timothy, Brian, Cheryl and Adam, Becky and Steve, and my precious grandchildren: Amanda, David O., Jessica and Andy, David R., Lauren R., Gabriel, Justin, Lauren, Ace, Dain, Tre', Patrick, Brooke, Paige and Emily, and my great-grandchildren: Dorian and Julian.

Acknowledgments

I want to express my appreciation to Lance Ivey, Director of the Heartland School of Ministry, for his assistance in reading and providing editorial feedback on the manuscript for this book. He willingly gave of his time with grace and kindness. His counsel helped bring this work to fruition. Also, a special thank you to Scott Albin, who read the draft and encouraged my heart. Thank you to Al Roever and Floyd Ellsworth, both pastors on staff at Heartland World Ministries Church in Irving, Texas, who read portions of the manuscript and offered their support as well.

To Jim Darnell: you are most special. I knew from our first conversation that your illustration for the cover would be fabulous.

How can I say enough thanks to my church fellowship group, who are a part of my church family and a real family to me. Your prayer covering had always been such a blessing to me.

From the very first inception of the idea for this book, Vicki McElroy, my dear friend, offered continual and positive encouragement. Thanks, Vicki, and to Estelle Jacklin, my precious friend, thank you for always supporting me.

I give a special thank-you and love to my husband, Frank, for his patience while I spent so much time at the computer.

Thank you also to my pastor, Steve Hill, of Heartland World Ministries Church, for his leadership, his example, and the "green light" he gave me.

To Janet Angelo, you were just what I needed in a copyeditor as well as a gift from God and a special jewel. Thank you so very much.

Finally, I give my utmost praise and thanksgiving to my creator, my heavenly Father, my Lord, and my best friend, Jesus. This work is from You and all about You, and You are the one to whom all credit, glory, and honor is due. What an amazing and gracious Savior! I give You my love and surrender. Thank You, Holy Spirit, for being my guide, inspiration, and power. Without You, the words could not have been written.

Table of Contents

Introduction	Designed for Greatness	xi
Chapter 1	Who Am I?	15
Chapter 2	Priceless Treasure	33
Chapter 3	Whose Business Are You Minding?	47
Chapter 4	Be Careful Little Eyes	69
Chapter 5	Be Careful Little Ears	79
Chapter 6	Be Careful Little Mouth	87
Chapter 7	How's Your Heart?	99
Chapter 8	En Garde!	113
Chapter 9	Plug in to the Power	125
Chapter 10	Melodies of Love	147
Chapter 11	Your Magnificent Machine	171
Chapter 12	Consider the Candle	179
Chapter 13	Shield or Rope: Which Will You Choose?	193

Introduction

DESIGNED FOR GREATNESS

*H*anging on and never giving up is a powerful force within us. I am reminded of a poster I saw several years ago. It showed a frenzied-looking kitten holding on to a thick rope with a big knot on the end. He looked like he had stuck his little paw into an electric socket, as his hair was standing on edge and he was clinging on to that rope for dear life. The caption: "Hang in there, Baby!" I identified with this picture and never forgot it. You see, I felt that way for years. My circumstances seemed very challenging to me, and the only thing I knew to do was to endure. At times I wanted out, but deep inside of me I knew I could never let go of my "rope" because I was not sure where I would fall. Are you at a place in your life now where you feel like you're barely hanging on?

In the pages of this book I will share the blessings that came to me because I did not give up, and also because I learned the right place to fall. The principles and truths I will share are life changing. I desire to place within you some nuggets of truth that you can "chew" on. They are like living seeds that, when dropped into the fertile soil of your mind, will grow and sprout into an abundant life, full of blessings. Someone dropped such seeds into my life through prayer on my behalf. Although it took some time for them to sprout, they bloomed forth in a mighty way. These marvelous principles did not become revelation knowledge to me sooner because of my own ignorance. The Word says, *"My people are destroyed for lack of knowledge"* ***(Hosea 4:9).***

This book is from my heart to yours. Precious one, *you* have such purpose and destiny. The Almighty God, the Creator of the Universe, designed you uniquely. You are loved! Do you know just how special you are? YES, wonderful things are in store for you if you will only believe and receive. I went for years not understanding that I was unconditionally loved. Maybe you feel that way right now. The enemy of your soul wants you to believe the lie that you are not loved. The truth, however, is that you *are* special and you *are* greatly loved just as you are.

Are you in the midst of trial and heartache? ***Don't give up.*** Have you been hurt and offended? ***Don't give up.*** Have others spoken of you with evil intent? ***Don't quit.*** Has life seemed to throw you a curveball? Are you allowing circumstances to pull you down? Maybe sickness has racked your body or depression has bombarded your mind. Are you grieving over the loss of your dearest friend or loved one? Does the financial pressure that plagues your life seem to be more than you can endure? Perhaps you are in the jaws of a powerful addiction. Or ... you have been the offender and you are plagued with guilt. My friend, do NOT be discouraged; instead, *NEVER GIVE UP.*

Why do we so frequently feel downcast and filled with despair? Can it be that we have not learned who we are (God's sons and daughters), and we have not learned how to trust Him for all things? Sometimes we just need someone to come alongside of us to love and teach us. There are answers for the trials of life. Those answers are coming your way. Yes, there are even miracles. I remind you, you're designed for purpose, greatness, and an abundant life. In your present situation, your "rope" may seem like a small thread, but don't despair — there is hope. Where there is an honest and searching heart, answers will come.

There is One who is always there when you let go! You must be willing to jump right into the net. I believe in miracles and the God of miracles. Do you want your miracle? Do you want to achieve your dream? It is there, waiting for you. You must reach out and receive.

"The world" measures success in terms of position, fame, money, and the power that money brings. How many people who have reached this ladder of success have succumbed to torment, loss of character and family, dreadful disease, or even suicide, among other things. We are most grateful to those who have used their resources to benefit mankind, but success can be elusive to many.

This book is not a study on "how to be successful in 12 easy steps." No, my precious friend, this is about the Master's Plan for your life, specifically designed with you in mind. When you commit the truths of these chapters to your life, you will be blessed and successful. You will learn how to choose to **NEVER GIVE UP**.

I want you to be blessed, for you are the purpose for this book. Stay with me to the very end. I will share what I learned that brought about dynamic change in my own life.

We are about to embark on a wonderful, life-changing journey.

Chapter 1

WHO AM I?

We have a perfect Creator who has placed within each of us unique creative gifts and qualities to be successful, not only so that we can be benefited, but also so that we can be a blessing to others. Every human born into this world has an innate desire within them to know who they really are, and they will never be satisfied until that knowledge is secure according to God's purposes.

In Psalm 8:4-8 we read, *"What is man, that thou art mindful of him? and the son of man, that thou visitest him? For thou hast made him a little lower than the angels and hast crowned him with glory and honour. Thou madest him to have dominion over the works of thy hands; thou hast put all things under his feet: All sheep and oxen, yea, and the beasts of the field; The fowl of the air, and the fish of the sea, and whatsoever passeth through the paths of the sea."* The word 'angels' in this passage means "a little lower than God – *elohiym* (el-o-heem)" in the Hebrew translation of the word.

Don't we take so much for granted? *"I will praise thee; for I am fearfully and wonderfully made"* **(Psalm 139:14).** *"So God created man in his own image, **in the image of God** created he him; male and female created he them"* **(Genesis 1:27).**

Please allow your mind to meditate upon these tremendous truths and begin to think of yourself as God thinks of you, for you are really something! The Lord is a Great God. He is a loving God who loves **YOU,** always and forever. He will never leave you or forsake you. *"Yea, I have loved thee with an everlasting love"* **(*Jeremiah 31:3*).**

What was true in my life could be true with you. For many years, I never really understood that the Heavenly Father loved me unconditionally. Throughout my life I struggled with feeling unloved. Not only did I feel unloved, but I also felt that I did not "measure up" and was always second best. Whatever I did was never good enough. I hear many similar stories from others who have struggled with these same feelings of inadequacy. I can tell you that for years I went through negative emotions because I did not understand who I was in Christ. Oh, I was very busy and seeking to do "good" as a committed Christian, but I was clueless about the real me. One day I came to understand that God loved me in a way I never dreamed possible. What liberating knowledge it was when I learned that God loved me no matter what I did or did not do.

Often people have a concept of God through their earthly relationship with their father. If there was a lack of feeling secure in that relationship, or their father was unable to express affection for them, it carries over into their adult life even if they become a Christian and know God loves them because the Bible says so. However, God's love is not like an earthly father's love, even if a man is a good father. Since loves never changes and He truly loves us the way we are, there is nothing that we can do to earn or merit His love. We absolutely cannot do anything to make Him love us more. God is all loving and all giving. It is His unchanging nature to be this way. It is most energizing and beneficial when we grasp the significance of this eternal truth in our life. It takes out the "work" of loving God and following Him, and it removes the "worry." When I accepted the undeniable truth of God's love, my outlook, as well as my entire life changed. I was transformed. I continue to learn about the abundant, victorious life available to me, all because I came to understand who I really was.

Let the eternal truth of God's Word sink deep into your soul so that inner healing can begin:

- *For God so **loved** the world, that he **gave** his only begotten Son, that whosoever believeth in him should not perish, but have everlasting life (**John 3:16**).*
- *For he hath said, I will never leave thee, nor forsake thee (**Hebrews 13:5**).*
- *But God, who is rich in mercy, for his great love wherewith he loved us (**Ephesians 2:4**).*
- *Behold, what manner of love the Father hath bestowed upon us, that we should be called the sons of God (**1 John 3:1**).*
- *But God commendeth his love toward us, in that, while we were yet sinners, Christ died for us (**Romans 5:8**).*

**God loved. God gave. God keeps on loving.
God keeps on giving.**

You see, my precious friend, Jesus has done it all for us. Yes, everything we need in this life has already been accomplished and we must learn how to appropriate the necessary ingredients for success. Note this scripture in Galatians 1:4: *"Jesus gave himself for our sins, that he might deliver us from this present evil world, according to the will of God and our Father."* This scripture describes the key to individual success in this world today. Maybe you are saying, "I'm not sure that makes sense." As we walk together through the pages of this book, I believe you will come to understand it fully.

Let us turn from the created one back to the Creator for a moment. There are so many awesome passages of Scripture about Jehovah God, but I would like to share with you verse 12 of Isaiah 40: *"Who hath measured the waters in the hollow of his hand, and meted out heaven with the span, and comprehended the dust of the earth in a measure, and weighed the mountains in scales, and the hills in a balance?"*

I had never heard a lesson or sermon preached on this passage of Scripture, yet when I first read these words, it demonstrated to me a dramatic picture of what a mighty God we serve.

I was raised in the Pacific Northwest on the Puget Sound. I was surrounded by water, and I developed a deep love for the seas, lakes, and rivers of that region. I never tired of watching the ferryboats from Seattle and the naval ships coming into the port of our town. To walk down to a sandy shore and take in the beauty of God's nature always had such a calming effect on me. I so enjoyed the water.

Mountains became another natural wonder for me. On a clear day we could see Mt. Rainier from our yard. When I moved to Alaska, I experienced the breath-taking experience of flying over those majestic, magnificent peaks. We also lived in Colorado Springs where every day I could look out my window and take in the splendid mountain range of the Rockies. I loved to drive up the winding mountain roads and look down over the towns and valleys below. All of this instilled in me a very awe-inspiring appreciation of the marvelous creations of God. I will tell you, I missed the mountains when we moved to Texas. But, more importantly, my love for the mountains and seas eventually made the words of this verse from God's Word become vividly and fully alive to me.

In this passage we see that God holds "the waters or all the seas" in the hollow of His hands. What a magnificent truth! It's almost too marvelous to comprehend. When we scoop up water and try to hold it in our hands, all that remains is about a tablespoon.

God measures the heavens with the span of His hand. How incredible this is, considering that the span of a human hand is about nine inches!

This verse also tells us that God comprehended the dust of the earth in a measure. What a God! I can't even capture the dust I shake off my dust cloth!

God weighs the mountains in scales, and the hills in a balance. My feelings for the beloved Mt. Rainier and the Rocky Mountains pale in comparison to this last statement within verse 12 of Isaiah 40. That God can do this is so far beyond our finite ability to understand. This is the same God who spoke the world into existence and breathed into man the breath of life so that man became a living soul. How can we possibly doubt anything that He can do?

Thinking of such glories can overwhelm us and cause us to feel unworthy of being loved by such an awesome God. It is true that we cannot merit eternal life in heaven in any other way than through Jesus' work on the cross. We have no goodness to give; money will not buy it; being a good person is just not good enough; our religious background carries no weight; a Christian heritage is not a sure guarantee. Even a casual decision in a church may not be a true salvation experience. Even being actively involved in church, though it is a good thing, is not a salvation experience. We can never do enough good works to qualify us for eternal life in heaven.

There is not one person on the face of the earth good enough to go to heaven on his own merit. We are all sinners and found to be absolutely guilty before God. The only way anyone gets to heaven is by way of the cross of Jesus Christ.

- *For all have sinned, and come short of the glory of God **(Romans 3:23)**.*
- *The wages of sin is death; but the gift of God is eternal life through Jesus Christ our Lord **(Romans 6:23)**.*
- *For by grace are ye saved through faith; and that not of yourselves: it is the gift of God **(Ephesians 2:8)**.*
- *With men it is impossible, but **not** with God: for with God all things are possible **(Mark 10:27)**.* This verse in the Amplified version reads: *For with God nothing is ever impossible and no word from God shall be without power or impossible of fulfillment.*

No, precious one, there is only one way to have salvation, redemption, and a heavenly home. Jesus Christ, the marvelous King of kings and Lord of lords, left heaven's glory and became a man, God in the flesh. He was the sinless, perfect Son of God who suffered, died, and shed His blood on the old rugged cross. The beautiful Jesus hung on a cross, marred by my sin, your sin, and the sin of the entire human race. Oh, the agony and suffering of that cross – just for me and just for you. The suffering for sin was so intense that He became unrecognizable. Let your mind grasp this. He arose the third day from the dead, victorious over death, hell, and the grave, to give us new life in Him. He *"was made to be sin for us, who knew no sin; that we might be made the righteousness of God in him"* **(2 Corinthians 5:21)**.

We must understand, first and foremost, that we are sinners in need of a "great exchange," so to speak. Jesus gave for you and me. Jesus loved supremely. He alone was qualified to be the perfect sacrificial Lamb, slain for the sins of the world. We must repent of our sins, since it was our sins that cost Him His life-blood. We receive salvation through repentance and calling upon the name Jesus Christ to save us and cleanse us from all our sin. We are told in the Word that unless we repent we **shall perish.** Repent means to turn from our old life and way of doing things and to allow Jesus to be Lord of our life. It encompasses **more** than being sorry for our sins. We must **change** from what we were doing to walk a new path. Our life was once in complete disorder, but when we receive Jesus, who is the God of order, He will put order and new life into us. Jesus is the Way, the Truth, and the Life, and *"no man comes to the Father but by Him."*

To summarize, it is not church membership or good works that will save us from eternal death; it is becoming a new person in Christ by calling out to Him. It is more than a decision *per se* — rather, it is receiving new life and understanding that through the transaction of repenting and believing we now have the privilege of a personal **relationship** with an awesome, mighty God. The Word declares that He is our Savior and friend — meaning, when we choose to follow Him it is more than an experience or a casual decision; it is **relationship.** Take a moment to examine your own heart to see if you are trusting in a decision or church membership.

Stop right now, my friend, and *know that you know* that you have Jesus and His Spirit dwelling in you. **If you do not have that assurance; believe in this simple truth:** *"That if thou shalt confess with thy mouth the Lord Jesus, and shalt believe in thine heart that God hath raised him from the dead, thou shalt be saved. For with the heart man believeth unto righteousness; and with the mouth confession is made unto salvation"* **(Romans 10:9-10).**

What possible reason could keep you away from the One who can forgive you, cleanse you, and make you whole?

Jesus is here welcoming you with open arms, ready to pour out His amazing and abundant life in you. He knocks on the door of your heart. He longs to come in and reside within you for all eternity. He alone knows how to direct the course of your life here on this earth to bring you into a place of truly abundant living.

If your salvation is not secure, you can pray the simple sinner's prayer right now. There's no better time than the present:

"Jesus, I repent of my sins and ask you to forgive and cleanse me. Come into my heart and life and be my Lord and Savior. I believe in you and trust you to live your life through me on this earth and take me to Heaven when I die. Thank you Jesus."

There is no way that you can begin the journey of *knowing who you are* until this first step of receiving Christ has been taken. The rest of this book will not apply to you and you will be unable to comprehend or obtain successful results from applying its principles and truths. All humanity must come to God in this same way. It is an act of surrendering our unworthy life and receiving a new life, one that is worthy to be filled with God's Holy Spirit, in exchange.

Once you become a child of God, your perspective on the world changes, and you become even more than you may have been before that God often gets a bad rap from the human race. He is blamed for sickness, calamities, natural disasters and much more that does not come from Him. God is not the problem. It is our natural bent on sinning that we inherited from our first parents – Adam and Eve. The Original Evil Instigator of Sin was Satan – the father of all lies — who is the Great Deceiver; he wants to kill, steal, and destroy every human being. The devil wants you to fail, and he works tirelessly to keep you in ignorance. We will discuss in a later chapter what brought about his demise.

The Bible, on which we base the entire premise for this road to success, declares to us:

- God cannot lie. (**Numbers 23:19; Romans 3:4; Hebrews 6:8**)

- There is no sin or darkness in God. **(James 1:17; Psalms 27:1; 1 John 1:5)**
- His Word is absolutely sure and true. **(Luke 21:33; Ezekiel 12:25; Psalms 111:7; Matthew 5:11)**

Again, with truth before us, how can we doubt God? God is awesome, mighty, and powerful. It is much easier to believe that God created man and that He created a tree for man to sit under than it is to believe the evolutionist theory! God declares in His magnificent Word that *"With men it is impossible, but not with God: for with God all things are possible"* **(Mark 10:27).** What a promise! What hope this gives us! I have seen some impossible things become possible in my life. We can totally trust in whatever He tells us to do.

Let us now consider who we are and how we are put together.

Every human being is a body, soul, and spirit. *"I pray God your whole spirit and soul and body be preserved blameless unto the coming of our Lord Jesus Christ"* **(1 Thessalonians 5:2).** When the truth of this scripture gets into your soul, it will affect your entire being. Our Creator is most concerned about who you are as a complete person. God wants you to be whole, healthy, and full of vitality.

Your body, which could also be termed your earth suit, houses the "real you." The body is designed for long and efficient use, but in reality it is often neglected and thus wears out and dies earlier than the original intent our Maker had for it. God wants us to keep it healthy and strong throughout our years. Often our bodies are neglected on the inside because we place too much emphasis on our outward appearance. Personally, I look forward to that marvelous day when we receive our resurrected bodies in heaven! However, in the meantime, aren't we glad that we have one now – a body that is. Women would have a hard time going shopping without having an earth suit needing to be clothed!

This body does not belong to us. When we become a Christian it belongs to Jesus. We will learn in a following chapter how to care for the body so that it will service us greatly throughout our life. God declares in His Word that our bodies are very important to him. He designed them with purpose. We should honor and revere our body and see to it that we do not destroy it.

In Romans 12:1 the Apostle Paul is telling us that we are to present our bodies as a *living* sacrifice, which means dying on a daily basis to self. There must be a beginning point, but every day we need to *reckon* an "I die daily" commitment to the Lord. Let us look at the meaning of the Greek Word *Zao* – "living: to live, breathe, be among the living, not lifeless, not dead; to enjoy real life; to have true life and be worthy of the name; (active, blessed, endless in the kingdom of God), living water, having vital power in itself and exerting the same upon the soul; to be in full vigor, to be fresh, strong, efficient."

We are to be a Divine representation of the Living God. I don't know about you, but I am not so inclined to want to listen to someone who is lifeless and emaciated telling me about the power of God. The purpose of our entire body, soul, and spirit is to represent the vital, powerful life of Jesus to a needy world.

Our soul (which is often referred to as our *heart* in the Bible) is our mind, will, and emotions. Too often we put great emphasis on our *head* knowledge or intellect. God calls this *carnal* knowledge. Still another way of putting it would be our *sense* knowledge or what we hear, see, smell, taste, and touch. Our knowledge comes from our learning experiences, which include our schooling, our environment, and our life experiences as well as everything we take into our brain and subconscious mind.

Each of us is given a free will to choose and make our own decisions. We were not created to be puppets. God Himself gave us free will, even though He knew that by exercising it we could get ourselves into a whole lot of trouble! The problems of life generally come from our own choices rather than choosing God's way. He wants us to choose Him and His way.

Another aspect of our makeup that we seem to rely on much more than we should is **our emotions**. God gave us wonderful emotions. Wouldn't it be terrible if we went around being stoic and purely logical all the time? But emotions, wrongly used, can get us into real difficulties. We simply cannot make decisions based on them. By nature, we want to *feel* it, whatever *"it"* may be to you. If circumstances are going well for us, then we are happy. As soon as the circumstances become overwhelming or full of crisis, however, and our feelings of joy seem to fly out the window. Living by faith does not mean going by our emotions or feelings, but instead, faith means believing in and acting upon the authoritative Word of God. Right decisions will bring a corresponding feeling of peace, contentment, and joy. There is a little saying that is very true:

> Feelings come and feelings go,
> Feelings are quite deceiving.
> Only faith based on God's Word
> Is really worth receiving!

The real you dwells within your **spirit** – who you are inside – also referred to in the Bible as your **inner man**. Your spirit man will live eternally either in heaven with your Creator and Savior Jesus Christ, or forever separated from Him in a never-ending hell; where you will spend eternity is governed by *your* choice. When I began to realize that the real me is my spirit (and not my body and emotions), and that the Holy Spirit actually dwells within my spirit, I began to understand why the Word makes such statements as: "I have the mind of Christ;" "I am complete in Him;" "I am to be perfect as my Father is perfect;" and, "It is not I, but Christ living in me."

God did not intend to put us here on this earth, give us the exchanged life, and then say, "Hey man, you are on your own; do the best you can and it will all work out in the end." No. He gave us His Word for direction. (You will find this repeated over and over again because it is His knowledge that we need.) When we are born again, the Holy Spirit is now in our life working within us and through us. This life is not about *"me"* and what *"I"* can do, but rather, it is about relinquishing ourselves and allowing Jesus to do the "working out" in our life. This is true for every child of God. This is the *key*, the *secret,* and the *answer* to successful living. We must ask God to reveal it to us by His Holy Spirit.

What we do in this life on earth will be in preparation for our eternal destiny (which hopefully will be in heaven). If we do not make the proper decisions now and instead choose to ignore the eternal consequences, there will be a price to pay – much higher and more severe than you could ever imagine. Remember, if you have *not* asked Jesus to enter into your spirit and take control of your life, you have secured an eternal destination that you would never deliberately choose if you had the chance to visit there first to see what it's like. Thankfully, God's grace allows us to make a change in our lives before it's too late. No one is out of God's reach of redemption and restoration.

When a person accepts Jesus Christ, the Holy Spirit actually takes up residence in the spirit of that person. The Holy Spirit is the One who brings about the change within you. It is a marvelous phenomenon. There is a throne within our inner man, and again, we determine who reigns on that throne, whether it is self or God. We must always remember that our spirit is who we really are, not our body and our mind. Either the flesh will be in control of us or the Holy

Spirit will be in control. It is the spirit of man that needs the most attention. God speaks into and through our spirit. We cannot do the work of God in our *sense knowledge*. It is the Holy Spirit operating through our spirit who brings life.

I think one of the most powerful scriptures in the Bible is Romans 8:11: *"But if the Spirit of him that raised up Jesus from the dead dwell in you, he that raised up Christ from the dead shall also quicken your mortal bodies by his Spirit that dwelleth in you."* Think on this for a moment. Read it again. Think of Calvary. Look at yourself. This is powerful. If we let this verse get down into our heart, it will bring dramatic results. I trust you are getting the picture of who you really are. It took a supernatural level of power to raise Jesus from the dead. My friend, God says that same power is within every believer! If you want to live above the normal and within the realm of that dynamic level, read and re-read Romans chapter 8, and when you couple it with the 6th chapter of Romans you have the heart of the gospel.

As stated earlier, God does not force us to believe in Christianity as though we are puppets. We accept and believe by our own choice. We must fully understand, however, that the Bible tells us there is a war between the flesh and the Spirit. The bad news for us is that our flesh – which includes our self-knowledge and emotions – is "carnal" or enmity (an enemy) against God. The flesh does not like the things that are holy. The flesh is self-centered. This old flesh – religious flesh, prettied-up flesh, Sunday-go-to-church flesh, moral flesh, be-kind-to-your-neighbor flesh, good-looking flesh or any other kind flesh – is still an enemy to God. It is *only* what we do through and by the Holy Spirit that is pleasing to our Lord. Life will take on a new dimension and *success* as we practice seeing through the eyes of God. That dynamite power will blow all of the little wimpy demons (that try to hinder you) right out your front door!

In all simplicity, all choices stem from either our inner carnal man or spiritual man. There is no in-between or gray area. One or the other rules us at any given moment throughout our lives. There is a constant war going on between the flesh and the Spirit.

Let us take a closer look at the meaning of the word *flesh*, which comes from the Greek word *sarx*, which means: "mere human nature, the early nature of man apart from divine influence, thus prone to sin and opposed to God." (This definition matches how the word *sarx* is used in the original Greek translation of Romans 8:1-9 and Romans 7:5, 18-19)

The flesh must be put down, but how do we do this? The Apostle Paul provided us with an answer to this question in Romans 6:11: "Likewise **reckon** (think, consider, and take into account) yourselves to be dead indeed unto sin, but alive unto God through Jesus Christ our Lord." The word 'reckon' comes from the Greek word *logizomai*. The meaning of this word has to do with what is actual reality. Our inner battle is in our thought life and the *reality* of the Spirit. As long as we "consider ourselves to be dead to sin" then the flesh has no control over us. Our spirit is in control. Furthermore, Romans 12:1-2 tells us how this is done: *by transforming of our mind through reading the Word of God on a **DAILY** basis.* Jesus paid the price for our sin at Calvary, and His blood purchased our redemption. Yes, we are saved, justified, preserved, healed, delivered, and made whole. It is all ours to claim. However, once we have experienced salvation, we must *reckon* it to be so by faith and claim our inheritance and victory continually. Always remember, sin is in opposition to God. (Here comes choice again!)

The good news: The Holy Spirit will be our Great Enabler, helping us understand our mind and sense knowledge in relation to our inner man and spirit as we go about the challenges of daily living.

God is who He says He is, and God will do what He says He will do: God's Word is forever settled in heaven. Let's take a few moments to meditate on the following powerful statements and the verses of scripture that support them:
I am who God says I am. I am where God says I should be. I have what God says I have, and I can do what God says I can do. This is true regardless of my feelings or my physical appearance.

- I am a new creation born of God. (**2 Corinthians 5:17**)
- I can overcome the world because God dwells within me. (**1 John 5:4**)
- I am an overcomer through the blood of the Lamb and the word of my testimony. (**Revelation 12:11**)
- I have been redeemed from the curse of the Law. (**Galatians 3:13**)
- I am accepted among the beloved and I am a joint-heir with Jesus Christ. (**Ephesians 1:6; Romans 8:17**)
- I am God's wonderful workmanship. (**Ephesians 2:10**)
- I am more than a conqueror through Christ who loves me. (**Romans 8:17**)
- I am strong in the Lord and in the power of His might. (**Ephesians 6:10**)
- Just as Jesus is, so am I in this world. (**1 John 4:17**)
- I was delivered from the power of darkness and put into the kingdom of Light. (**Colossians 1:13**)
- I have access to the God's throne room and can see people and things from His vantage point. (**Ephesians 1:21-23**)
- I have authority over the enemy. (**Luke 10:19**)
- I have a complete set of spiritual armor. (**Ephesians 6:13-18**)

- I have wisdom available to me 24/7. (**James 1:5**)
- All of God's resources are available to me. (**1 Corinthians 3:21-23; 2 Peter 1:3-4**)
- I have been given faith that all things are possible for me. (**Hebrews 12:2; Mark: 23**)
- I can be full of love, joy, peace, patience, gentleness, goodness, faith, meekness, and self-control through the Spirit. (**Galatians 5:21**)
- I can do all things through Christ who strengthens me. (**Philippians 4:13**)
- I am victorious. (**1 Corinthians 15:57**)

Let us take a little side trip that is most revealing about the nature of Jesus, which is important in understanding who we are in Him. If you will go to chapters 14, 15, 16, and 17 of the Gospel of John and circle the **"I's"** spoken by Jesus Christ, you will learn much of His purpose on this earth. For instance, He states, "I Am, I come, I speak, I have done, I will send, I declare, I will show, I will come back," and so on. When we read the actions that follow the pronoun "I" spoken by Jesus, it helps us understand what He did for us and what He desires for us. He wants to live freely within us. The success of our life was guaranteed at Calvary where Jesus provided His exchanged Life for us. With this knowledge we should *never give up* until the day we are gloriously taken out of this present world and brought into the eternal presence of His Majesty, King of kings and Lord of lords. **True success means having the Lord Jesus at the helm of our life,** for He has *"given unto us all things that pertain unto life and godliness, through the knowledge of him..." (2 Peter 1:3).*

Knowing who we are is basic and vital in this journey of success. In the early chapters of this book we are laying a foundation in preparation for our journey, because in all good things there must be preparation. Preparation comes about through the right thinking of who we are as well as through work, diligence, and a searching heart. There will always be challenges, opposition, and trials. I would not tell you otherwise. Disappointments and failures are part of the road to success. Generally, we learn more from our failures. A truly successful person has learned to walk the avenues of humility and obedience. Learning takes effort and is truly *worth* the effort. Accomplishments are worth the investment in preparation. Isn't it great to know there is a fully proven way of accomplishing success? We do not have to constantly blunder. We are uniquely designed to live the abundant successful life in Jesus. Discipline is a key – discipline of the body, discipline of the Mind, discipline of the Soul, and discipline of the spirit! As the hymn writer has penned, "there is no other way but to trust and obey."

REVIEW

- You are a unique and special creation of Almighty God, designed for greatness.
- Are you determined to see yourself as God sees you, or do you want to remain in the status quo? It is your choice.
- God's love for you is based on His truth, which never changes – not by our feelings or actions.
- All that we need and will ever need in the future was accomplished by Jesus' completed work on Calvary. He gave us a new, exchanged life because of His supreme love for mankind. Knowing Jesus is the first step to success.
- Our awesome, creative God cannot lie. He is absolute truth and holiness.
- The Lord created us as triune beings having a body, soul, and spirit. The "real" me is the Holy Spirit dwelling in the inner man who was given at Salvation.

We are created to be a divine representation of God. We exercise our free will to choose whom we will serve, whether ourselves or the living Lord.

Take time to record what God has spoken to your heart as you've read this chapter and studied the scripture references provided so that you can review it later. Write down scripture(s) that you want to remember and use in your daily walk.

In the next chapter we'll discover that all of these truths are hidden within a **priceless treasure** that God has already given to us.

Chapter 2

PRICELESS TREASURE

My son, *if you receive my words, and treasure my commands within you, so that you incline your ear to wisdom, and apply your heart to understanding; yes, if you cry out for discernment, and lift up your voice for understanding, if you seek her as silver, and search for her as for hidden treasures; then you will understand the fear of the LORD, and find the knowledge of God* **(Proverbs 2:1-5 NKJV)**.

A good man out of the good treasure of the heart bringeth forth good things: and an evil man out of the evil treasure bringeth forth evil things **(Matthew 12:35)**.

The Greek word *thesauros* means **treasure**, transliterated: the place in which good and precious things are collected and laid up; receptacle in which valuables are kept; a treasury; storehouse, repository of collected treasures.

Noah Webster's original dictionary written in 1828 gives some great definitions for **treasure**. (By the way, today's versions of the dictionary cannot compare with his original, exhaustive work). **Treasure**: "A great quantity of any thing collected for future use; something very much valued; great abundance; repository." According to Mr. Webster, the mind or memory is called the repository of ideas.

I have five children. It would have been nice if each child had arrived with a manual of instructions tied to his/her ankle titled, "How to Raise this Child to 18 Years of Age." I certainly spent enough time in 'trial and error' and more error than I care to think about.

God gave us a manual containing instructions in righteousness so that we may know Him and know exactly what He expects of us. Within its pages there is an answer for every problem that we will ever encounter in this life. Every subject we need to know is addressed within its pages; it is a manual without error and is always true.

This manual is also a perfect songbook for praise and worship, particularly the book of Psalms. Furthermore, this manual is very personal; it speaks so individually to each of our hearts that it's like we've been given a personal love letter from God Himself. This manual is the Holy Bible, the living, breathing Word of God, the Holy Scriptures, and truly it is a **priceless treasure**. It should have an honored place in your life. Your love for the Lord is expressed and reflected by how much you spend reading it.

The Bible is not a book to be dusted off and carried to church on Sunday morning. It is vital, relevant, and necessary to our success. It is also more than a priceless treasure; the Bible is a powerful weapon. The Bible, God's Holy Word, is the Book of the Ages, which never becomes outdated or obsolete.

When we put the Word in us we are putting God's love in our hearts. **Consider the power of the following scriptures about the Book of the Ages:**

- *So shall my word be that goeth forth out of my mouth: it shall not return unto me void, but it shall accomplish that which I please, and it shall prosper in the thing whereto I sent it **(Isaiah 55:11)**.*

- *For ever, O LORD, thy word is settled in heaven (**Psalm 119:89**).*
- *The grass withereth, the flower fadeth: but the word of our God shall stand for ever (**Isaiah 40:8**).*
- *For thou hast magnified thy word above all thy name (**Psalm 138:2**).*
- *Is not my word like as a fire? saith the LORD; and like a hammer that breaketh the rock in pieces? (**Jeremiah 23:29**)*
- *In the beginning was the Word, and the Word was with God, and the Word was God (**John 1:1**).*
- *For the prophecy came not in old time by the will of man: but holy men of God spake as they were moved by the Holy Ghost (**2 Peter 1:21**).*
- *I will hasten my word to perform it (**Jeremiah 1:12**).*
- *Jesus answered and said unto them, Ye do err, not knowing the scriptures, nor the power of God (**Matthew 22:29**).*

God distinctively told Moses in Deuteronomy 6:5 that he was to obey God's voice and keep His covenant with the promise that Moses would be a unique *treasure* above all people.

In the longest chapter of the Bible, which is Psalm 119 with its 176 verses, the Scriptures are referred to 174 times as the Word, testimonies, commandments, statutes, ways, judgments, precepts, or law." This Book is very important to God!

Why then, is there such struggle and opposition within human hearts to read this matchless Book – The Holy Bible – and seek eternal wisdom and truth within its pages? Why do so many of God's children know so little of it? The enemies of God, Satan and his wicked demons, know that within the glorious pages of the Book called the Holy Scriptures there is life – living, breathing words that tell of redemption and life-changing truths. The Holy God of the universe dictated

His Word to godly men, and it has the power to liberate and expose all of the enemy's evil purposes. Naturally, then, the devil will do anything and everything to keep anyone from its pages.

Of course, we have to consider the battle of the flesh and the spirit. Our old flesh doesn't want to be told what to do.

We can no more function properly and live expectantly in victory without the infusion of the Word deep into our souls than a professional can function without his tools. We must make a decision to know the Bible's content. The Holy Spirit uses the Word that we put into us for our growth, blessing, and victory. It is like putting seed into good soil. If we do not put the Word of God in us, we limit God and ourselves. The Bible is our comfort, peace, praise, and thanksgiving; our guide for life and our weapon of warfare against the enemy. The Word is Jesus and Jesus is the Word. To read and learn the Word is to know the heart of God.

Any study of the Scripture would have to include this powerful verse: *"For the word of God is quick, and powerful, and sharper than any two-edged sword, piercing even to the dividing asunder of soul and spirit, and of the joints and marrow, and is a discerner of the thoughts and intents of the heart"* ***(Hebrews 4:12).***

Dr. Aiko Hormann, who is a brilliant scientist and Bible teacher, said the Lord gave her revelation knowledge about Hebrews 4:12: "The Word is like a laser beam." I researched the definition of laser beam on the Internet and found the following: "A very intense beam of light of one color made by putting energy into a material." We know that the laser beam can cut and heal, among many other things, which is a very interesting thought. I also liked Dr. Aiko's favorite saying: "Science is catching up with the Bible."

A field of scientific research called cymatics studies the relationship of sound and physical reality as well as the impact sound has on matter. This field of study has particular interest regarding the spoken Word of God. I first read about this in the March 2007 issue of the *Mishpochah* newsletter, which is a publication of the ministry of Sid Roth. The title of this particular article was "Hebrew, the Language from Heaven," written by Alyosha Ryabinov. He wrote the following statement: "Hans Jenny was a Swiss physician and scientist who constructed an instrument called a "tonoscope" to make sound visible on substances like water or sand. Different shapes appeared on the sand as the result of different sounds coming through the device. He then tried spoken words in different languages but nothing happened. When he spoke the Hebrew language, however, the language spoken made the shapes of Hebrew vowels on the sand. None of the modern languages did that." This tells us there is power in the Word when it's spoken in Hebrew!

I am fairly certain if you are reading this book that you have a Bible. If not – run to the nearest Christian bookstore and invest in one. What honor do you place in your Bible? What does it really mean to you? Does it have unspeakable value to your heart? Your answers will reveal your relationship to the Master Teacher and Savior, Jesus

Where would a doctor be without his diagnostic tools and instruments? Would you want him to operate on you with dirty hands? Would you want a painter to come to your home without bringing his brushes, or would you be comfortable flying in a plane with a pilot who had flunked out of his flight training and had no working knowledge of the cockpit? We would not knowingly trust ourselves to a taxi driver who did not have a license. How long would one last on a new job if he was not willing to take the training and instruction required to learn a new position? A soldier could go all the way through boot camp and become trained and prepared for war with his combat gear ready, but if he was called into battle, just how far would he get if he didn't put the ammo in the gun?

We could take the same train of thought and apply it to the Christian who does not have a "working" knowledge of the Word of God. We do not want to be ineffective as believers. It is important for us to know how to apply Scripture to our everyday life. The lack in this skill became very apparent to me when I was working as a prayer counselor for a Christian television network. I was amazed at how many Christians, including leaders, did not know how to apply God's Word to obtain victory over difficult circumstances in their lives.

The Word of God is seed. All life comes from seed. The farmer plows up the soil and prepares it because he wants a great crop of corn. My friend, it goes without saying that unless the farmer puts corn seed in the fertile ground, he will never have a crop of corn. The Word (or Seed) of God must be planted into our mind for us to have a "spiritual harvest." There are promises for every need we'll encounter in our earthly life, but how can we pray specifically and with impact unless we know the portion of scripture that can be applied to meet those needs?

I have 3 x 5 cards with scripture verses written on them placed throughout my home – in the bedroom, bathroom, living room, and kitchen – and even in my car. I often have a CD of spoken Scripture playing in my computer. I play Scripture on my DVD and MP3 player. I do this because the Bible is life, and I need to have life flowing into me continually. If we are called upon to pray for others, we need to know what the Word says. Seed produces fruit. The beauty of seeds is that they always give us a greater amount of fruit and vegetables in proportion to what is planted.

The key to making the Bible come alive in your life is to *meditate* on the Word. In the Hebrew language the word "meditate" means "to muse, moan, speak, or utter." The English meaning is "to think on; to revolve in the mind."

Meditating brings the God-breathed Word to your heart, also known as the *rhema* Word. This is when a scripture seems to leap off the page of the Bible and go right to the heart. The power of the *rhema* Word becomes very apparent when that particular scripture is applied to our life. The *rhema* Word becomes rooted in us. It is a blessing while reading the Bible (*Logos,* meaning the written Word) when we can receive a *rhema* Word directly from God. The Lord says that we are to ask and allow Him to teach us. *"Teach me to do thy will; for thou art my God: thy spirit is good; lead me into the land of uprightness"* ***(Psalm 143:10).*** This should be our daily prayer. In Psalm 1:2 we are told to delight in the Word and to mediate in it day and night. Doing so will bring many benefits to our life:

- We will have a strong foundation.
- We will bring forth fruit in our life.
- We will be unfading.
- We will prosper in whatever we do.

Joshua 1:8 says that we are to meditate in the Word day and night and not allow it to depart out of our mouth; instead, we're to *observe all that is written therein.*

First Timothy 4:15 speaks of meditating with the idea of ***pondering, attending to carefully, and caring for.*** He exhorts us to give ourselves wholly to the instructions found within the Word. Everyone profits through the study and meditation of the Bible.

Meditating on the Word is the true path to success, because doing so encourages us to *never give up.* I would like to suggest reading the Bible aloud. Remember the scripture, *"Faith cometh by hearing and hearing by the Word of God"* ***(Romans 10:17).*** If you just casually read the Bible, you will find that your mind will wander and thus you will not receive the richness of what God wants for you. Reading the Word out loud will help keep your mind focused. Rich blessings come into our lives when we hear the Word, receive it, and act upon it.

There are some things you can do to make the Bible your own personal treasure. Personalize it by replacing the words "I" and "you" in particular scripture verses that speak to you, and instead write in your own name. This makes those scriptures come alive to you and speak to your heart. Remember: God's Word is a love letter written just for you. Our own knowledge and effort will never be the source of true success, peace, and victory. Those must come from knowledge we obtain through the Holy Spirit.

In America we take so many little pleasures for granted; for instance, having access to a wonderful hot shower. How refreshing it is to step into a warm shower after a hard day of work or upon rising to start the day, clean and fresh. It is the same with being able to spend time in the presence of the Lord and to be cleansed by His Word. As long as we have the dirt of guilt, trauma, pride, fear, doubt and sin in our souls we will be unable to be the successful person God designed us to be. Anger, resentment, strife, hatred, strongholds, bitterness, hard-heartedness, lawlessness, rejection, inferiority, and all such spiritual entanglements are washed away under the influence of the powerful, life-changing language of the Eternal God. We can be forgiven, washed, restored, and made whole simply by believing and acting upon the Word that has already been given to us. It is never too late to start.

It is His promise that we are cleansed through His Word: *"Now ye are clean through the word which I have spoken unto you" (John 15:3).*

As we are cleansed, we are to continue in the things we have learned. Precious friend, it is very easy to be cleansed and then turn right around and go back into the same paths unless we continue in the daily walk of being instructed by God. The good news of successful living in Christ is the daily *reckoning* that produces the cleansing. Would you think about going five days without a bath? I suppose it can be considered normal in some parts of the world but not in the society in which most of us live. The result of such disregard for the cleanliness of our bodies would make us offensive to others. Our flesh is just as offensive to the Spirit and thus is totally unacceptable.

We all know there are certain laws and principles that are always in operation even if we do not see or heed them: the laws of gravity, aerodynamics, and electricity; what we sow we *will* reap; the sun comes up in the morning and sets at night; one day is 24 hours, and so on. Whether or not we consider and cooperate with these natural laws does not change the fact of their existence. They are always in operation. God's Word is unchangeable. His Words are true and precise. We can totally depend on God's laws and truths to do what He said they would do. We must listen to the warnings and admonitions as well as the promise. Consider what God says about His Word in this verse in Isaiah: *"So shall my word be that goeth forth out of my mouth: it shall not return unto me void, but it shall accomplish that which I please, and it shall prosper in the thing whereto I sent it" (Isaiah 55:11-12).*

What **P**romise, what **P**rovision, and what **P**ower are contained in those few words!

This is the reason why we should read the Word, thoroughly know the Word, speak out the Word, pray the Word, and use it as our Sword against the enemy. The Word does the work. It is not by our words (please refer to the 12th chapter of Matthew); but rather, God sent His Word to heal others of their destructions (see Psalm 107:20). The laser beam of His Word is powerful.

Let me give you an illustration of a man who determines his own reasoning. He is a foolish driver. While driving down a dark country road, he is suddenly confronted with a sign that reads: **Stop. Detour. Bridge Is Out.** The driver stops and then determines that everything looks fine from *his* vantage points. He does not heed the warning sign and continues to drive only to have the car plunge into an icy river. Aren't we like this at times? We don't stop and listen. We have a casual and even flippant attitude concerning things eternal, and when the warnings within God's Word are unheeded, we complain about the mess we've made of our lives.

So often the pattern of life is work, work, work. Busy, Busy, Busy! So much to do! Children and family need my attention! Problems and crises to deal with! We feel like little hamsters on a wheel – going round and round – unable to get off.

We hear it said that we do not have time to read the Bible. Did you know that the entire Bible can be read through in about sixty hours? When I first heard this it sparked my interest, so I did a little research for myself. I can read through the Book of Ephesians, aloud, with expression, in nineteen minutes. The Book of Philippians can be read in fourteen minutes, 1 Thessalonians in eight minutes, and Titus in five minutes.

Time flies by as we go through daily life. We will wake up one day and realize that we are spent, empty, and frustrated as well as sick and tired of being sick and tired. In the final analysis of it all, we find the cause rests in the fact that we have not lived in the reality of the power of the Word of Life.

Can you just imagine what would take place in the Christian community if God's children would turn off the TV and spend at least twenty to thirty minutes a day reading His Word instead? All it would take is to give up one TV program a day. I am absolutely certain that you will accomplish great things if you simply dedicate that time to the Lord. Think of all the "stuff" you would keep out of your mind.

Probably the least productive thing you can do for your child is to allow them to soak up secular TV before they go to bed. As parents, we are to be guardians of their minds. We can raise our children to be great readers, great musicians, and to have creative minds by directing their minds to the right sources of inspiration. I would say that also includes limiting video and TV games and activities outside the home.

The last thing you listen to before you go to sleep will stay in your subconscious mind throughout the night. It will also be what you're thinking of when you wake up.

I well remember the years of 1994 and 1995 when I was so bombarded with stress and problems that I could readily identify with the little hamster who spends his time going round and round in his little wheel and can't seem to get off. I was on running on empty and totally drained. I hit a colossal burnout. Our precious God, in His grace, allowed me to get away and begin to find Him in the midst of all the mess. Thus began a progressive journey of searching until I found what I needed. More accurately, the Lord was positioning me to receive the powerful promises and truths of His Word so that I no longer had to live with a sense of rejection, heartache, and the emptiness of life. At the time I was spending almost every day in church or church-related activity, but in comparison, I was spending little time searching the Scriptures to find the answers for my needs. How pitiful – being busy in church but too tired for the Word! The good news is that I was about to personally learn the marvelous reality of the exchanged life in Christ that I had been longing for. Yes, that life is found in the Word.

It is not the hours you spend in church and being involved in church activities or the time you spend doing good deeds that will make a difference in your life. All of these activities should be a by-product of the time you've already spent with the Lord in His Word. It is the knowledge of the Scriptures that will transform you. This transformation will then spill over and bless others. God always honors His Word.

The Bible is not confusing, impractical, or outdated. On the contrary, dear friend, it takes away the confusion, depression, hurts, struggles, and heartaches as we apply it to our hearts and actions.

We live in a hurried and demanding society, and it is easy to become weary. However, we have been given this promise in the Word: *"They that wait upon the L*ORD *shall renew their strength; they shall mount up with wings as eagles; they shall run, and not be weary; and they shall walk, and not faint"* **(Isaiah 40:31)**. When we are in need of wisdom, we can find the answer to our search in this verse: *"If any of you lack wisdom, let him ask of God, that giveth to all men liberally, and upbraideth not; and it shall be given him"* **(James 1:5)**.

There are hundreds of precious promises found within the pages of the Bible. We live in an imperfect world, but praise God, as His children, we *can* live the life in Christ even though we're in this present evil world, and we can do so by the power of His Word and the assistance of the Holy Spirit. This is actually the normal way to live, meaning, the way God planned it from the beginning before Adam and Eve sinned in the Garden of Eden. He created us to have perfect communion with Him. Anything else is an abnormal way to live.

My pastor, Steve Hill, is always saying, "Don't go through the Bible; instead, let the Bible go through you." The essence of what he's saying can be found in this scripture: *"Teach me to do thy will; for thou art my God: thy spirit is good; lead me into the land of uprightness"* **(Psalm 143:10)**.

My Bible is my most prized possession. I am continually amazed at how it speaks to my heart. There are times when I cannot go beyond a single verse because of the truths and lessons I am learning from it or the reminders I receive. I hear, see, and feel God in its pages. It changes me. It is very easy to understand why Satan constantly works to keep people from knowing the Bible. He knows the power of its light and life.

I would encourage you to become a student of the marvelous teaching in this Precious Treasure—God's Word—the Holy Bible. As you read it, imagine yourself seated at the feet of the Master Teacher, Jesus himself. Furthermore, encourage your own heart by *meditating* on the Word day and night. I encourage you to memorize the following scriptures, as they will be a great source of strength to you:

All scripture is given by inspiration of God, and is profitable for doctrine, for reproof, for correction, for instruction in righteousness: That the man of God may be perfect, thoroughly furnished unto all good works **(2 Timothy 3:16-17)***.*

Apply thine heart unto instruction, and thine ears to the words of knowledge **(Proverbs 23:12)***.*

For all the promises of God in him are yea, and in him Amen, unto the glory of God by us **(2 Corinthians 1:20)***.*

REVIEW

- The priceless treasure of God's Word is ours, waiting to be opened in order to reveal the riches that are ours to claim for an abundant and fruitful life.
- We can trust every word within the Bible to be true and pure, faultless, applicable to every need we experience, and full of victory, power, and authority.
- It is the sure Word of defeat to the enemy of our soul.
- The Word is like a seed to be planted in the fertile soil of our mind.
- Remember: The Word will keep us from sin, or sin will keep us from the Word.
- To fully understand the precepts and depths of this priceless treasure we must be endued with the power of the Holy Spirit.

- Will you begin today, to give it top priority to the study of the Bible in your daily walk?

Now that we have examined the importance of the Scriptures, God's holy Word, we will learn in the next chapter how to bring our mind into submission to His Word so that we can be effective in our walk with the Lord and as a witness to others.

Chapter 3

WHOSE BUSINESS ARE YOU MINDING?

*E*very action first begins with a thought. Do we really pay enough attention to our thought life? How many times have we said (or heard it said), "I'm sorry, I didn't mean to do that," or "I'm sorry, I didn't mean to say that." We think negative words and verbalize them without considering the consequences that will result. The bottom line is that the negative things we say were in our mind to begin with, and they came out from the heart by way of our mouth. Unfortunately, once our "mind has spoken," it is often difficult to retrieve those words.

Picture this: you are the executive assistant to the president of a company with all of his authority backing you up. Here comes an unwanted visitor (negative thought). You have the authority to say, "Visitor (Thought), I cannot let you in." Now, if the "visitor" (thought) pushes through, it has then become an "unwanted visitor," and you as the executive assistant have the right to escort the unwanted visitor to the door.

Our Word of Life says, *"For the weapons of our warfare are not carnal, but mighty through God to the pulling down of strong holds; Casting down imaginations, and every high thing that exalteth itself against the knowledge of God, and bringing into captivity every thought to the obedience of Christ" (2 Corinthians 10:4-5).* If we read the preceding verse, we learn that we are in warfare, but thankfully we *do* have the weapons available to us to fight off the enemy, who wants to infiltrate our minds with his damaging thoughts.

The one thing the enemy uses more than any other weapon is to attack our minds. If the devil is allowed to do so (by us), he can implant thoughts that we do not want, and those thoughts will give us more grief than we can ever handle unless we have discernment about the marvelous organ we call the brain and use caution with what we allow to come in and go out of it.

Too often, our mind is like a little rowboat out on the sea. It just drifts around and moves with every little wave that comes lapping against it. It is in motion without any destination. We allow our minds to drift without taking into account that it really isn't drifting, but rather, it is implanting random thoughts that will come through our sense knowledge. Like breathing, thinking is something that goes on within us all the time. We are not aware of the fact that we are constantly thinking! We are continually putting thoughts into our mind like inputting data into a computer. Therefore, our mind is always working for us or against us. Dr. Caroline Leaf states the following in her book *Who Switched Off My Brain?:* "At any one moment, the brain is creatively inputting about 400 billion actions, of which we are only conscious of about 2,000. We think about 20,000 thoughts per day and our brains have the storage capacity of 3 million years." The brain is quite marvelous! It is astounding to think that we only use about 1 to 8 percent of its capacity.

It is crucial for us to understand how the brain works physiologically as well as how the mind works. This material can change your life and the lives of those around you. We *must learn* to control our thoughts.

When you are happy, joyful, and at peace, thinking positive thoughts and saying positive words to others and ourselves, certain chemicals (neurotransmitters/endorphins) are released from your brain. Pleasurable feelings result, which makes those endorphins the best anti-depressive medication you can take!

The opposite is also true. When we dwell on painful memories, hurtful experiences, or think negative thoughts and words, we are putting negative pictures into our minds that are releasing powerful chemicals that will course through our body, spilling out poison and toxicity into our hearts, bones, blood supply, and immune system. This places stress on our bodies – every organ and cell of the body—creating all manner of sicknesses.

Researchers say that 87 percent to 92 percent of the illnesses that plague us today are a direct result of our thought life. Furthermore, Dr. Caroline Leaf states in her book that the body and mind are integrally connected. She expands on this by noting the following statistics: "According to the American Institute of Stress, between 75 to 95 percent of visits to primary care physicians are due to stress-related disorders. Negative reinforcement releases negative chemicals; positive reinforcement releases positive chemicals. Therefore, toxic thoughts produce toxic emotions, which produce toxic attitudes, resulting in toxic behavior." Dr. Leaf goes on to say that most people are surprised to learn that their thoughts, attitudes, habits, and emotions are largely responsible for their mental and physical health. Furthermore, it is not only what we think, but also what we hear and what we watch that impacts our health. "All these things are processed through the brain, and if the incoming data is negative, then toxic chemicals will be released. Positive thoughts can de-stress you. Our thoughts and emotions are linked together in the same way that our body and mind are." It is also interesting that Dr. Leaf also states that "**emotional perceptions are not reliable because they can misinterpret the truth: they mix truth and fact.**" How much trouble we get into because we *think* we are right on a certain issue and yet we do not have full knowledge of the facts!

I have been privileged to sit under the teaching of Dr. Aiko Hormann. Dr. Aiko is a scientist who has studied the brain and artificial intelligence. In her early working years she was employed at the Pentagon. From her testimony we learned that one of her peers challenged her to disprove, mathematically, the prophecies of the Bible. Of course she could not, and as a result she became a Christian and studied the Word of God with the same intensity as she had studied science. She is a powerful teacher of the Word, and she has a wealth of knowledge of how the mind works in correlation to the Bible. (After all, it was God who created the brain.) I learned so much from her. Dr. Aiko stated the same thing as Dr. Leaf, but she worded it this way: "Every thought and every feeling you experience is an electro-chemical event in your brain and nervous system, and it will have a physiological consequence. If it is negative, it will bring bio-chemical changes in your body."

In essence, what this is saying is that emotions such as unforgiveness, resentment, bitterness, guilt, anger, worry, anxiety, fear, frustration, and excessive grief can release a flood of destructive chemicals into the body causing such diseases as hypertension, heart attacks, strokes, migraine headaches, cancer, skin disease, allergies, infections, diabetes, fybromyalgia, asthma, autoimmune disorders, and more. Every organ and cell – including the nervous and digestive systems – will be negatively affected by negative emotions.

It is interesting to note that stress comes from fear. From Dr. Leaf's research we learn that fear triggers more than

1,400 known physical and chemical responses and activates more than thirty different hormones and neurotransmitters.

Dr. Leaf teaches that our thoughts fall into two categories: faith-based thoughts or fear-based thoughts. I like to refer to these as God-kind of thoughts or enemy-kind of thoughts.

The Word tells us to think on those things that are true, honest, just, pure, lovely, and of a good report (see Philippians 4:6). God's thoughts are happy thoughts of family, friends, and the special times we've shared with them, as well as thanksgiving in all things, praise, worship, faith, spiritual songs and hymns, the Word, and the Lord.

Negative thoughts – meaning, the enemy's kind of thoughts –include fear, pride, stress, worry, anxiety, doubt, unbelief, hurts, contention, unforgiveness, resentfulness, anger, rage, jealousy, evil thinking, and negative self-talk as we learned above.

Keep in mind what the Word says we are to do concerning thoughts influenced by the enemy: *"For though we walk in the flesh, we do not war after the flesh: For the weapons of our warfare are not carnal, but mighty through God to the pulling down of strong holds; casting down imaginations, and every high thing that exalteth itself against the knowledge of God, and bringing into captivity every thought to the obedience of Christ"* **(2 Corinthians 10:3-5).** (This is worthy repeating.) If the thought comes into your mind to speak a hurtful word, or you're taunted by the memory of hurtful things that have been said and/or done to you (which the enemy would love to have us dwell on), immediately pray, "Lord I cast this upon you, because you said I could do so according to 2 Peter 5:7." Thus, the thought that could be harmful is now given to the Lord. Or you can say, "In the name of Jesus and by the power of His blood – I tell this thought to go." You will feel the immediate release of peace that will flood your spirit.

I have only referenced two illustrations of how to handle negative or harmful thoughts. There are many other scriptures to use in fighting this battle. Remember, we are told to *resist* the enemy with the promise that he will flee from us. This applies to our thought life and words as well. The more we are consciously aware of what we are thinking, the easier it is to capture those thoughts and be in command of them. I would also like to add that we must lean on the Holy Spirit. Ask His help in this discipline. He will accomplish it within us. We need to ***think about what we are thinking!***

Memories both good and bad are stored in the brain. There are times when the bad memories surface and we are prone to react without realizing that we are doing so. Our emotions are set off. A sound, a voice, or a specific person can set off these memories. Dr. Aiko refers to these as "trigger mechanisms." For instance, we can become victim to traumas such as the horrors of war, a terrible accident, abuse of a physical, verbal or sexual nature, word curses, a difficult relationship, witnessing a frightening event, a terrifying incident, and so on, and later in life certain thoughts, words, expressions, sounds, or events can trigger this incident in our mind and bring it back to the surface of our conscious memory, thus creating more toxic chemicals to be released. We can add the following to the list of negative emotions that can have this sort of involuntary trigger effect: rejection, abandonment, feelings of being lost, darkness, financial problems, the lack of success and prosperity, false spirituality, fear, revulsion, rage, betrayal, hopelessness, despair, shame, humiliation— and this is to name just a few. The destructive power of whatever might fly out of our mouths compounds the problem. The good news is that we can be set free from hurtful memories through prayer, and then we can begin building good memories in their place so that when bad memories come up, they will not carry the former negative knee-jerk reactions that hurt us mentally, spiritually, and emotionally.

In her teachings Dr. Aiko has shared that at least 80 percent of our actions are motivated by unconscious inner needs and drives. We all have the basic human needs to be accepted, to feel worthwhile, and to feel capable at what we choose to do in our life's work. When these needs are unfulfilled, we tend to substitute them with something else. We need to recognize these problems within ourselves. Ask God to reveal to you the deeply buried root causes of your inner needs and drives.

I would like to share with you some prayers that Dr. Aiko uses in her booklet *Triggering Mechanisms*:

"Heavenly Father, in the name of Jesus, I ask You to move by Your Holy Spirit to reveal to me the root causes of my 'triggering mechanisms.'"

"Dear Holy Spirit, bring to me pictures, scenes of events, or persons when I speak the following words (choose from the list starting with *memories above)."

As a prayer of preparation:

"My Heavenly Father, I submit myself to You totally, spirit, soul and body, in the name of Jesus. I know Your mighty weapon is far greater than any stronghold of the enemy in my life. I ask You to mobilize Your ministering spirits on my behalf for this occasion, in Jesus' mighty name."

With authority, pray:

"I cancel and nullify the power of this event (experience from the list) in the name of Jesus Christ of Nazareth and by the power of the Holy Spirit. I cut the link between the outer stimuli and my inner reactions, in the name of Jesus Christ of Nazareth. I ask You, Lord Jesus, to establish a new link-in with Your personal presence."

"I command you spirits of darkness that came in with this experience and all other related spirits (fear, rejection, guilt, etc.) to go now, in the name of Jesus, and become part of the footstool of Jesus Christ of Nazareth."

Remember we have the authority God gave us according to Luke 10:19: "Behold, I give unto you power to tread on serpents and scorpions, and over all the power of the enemy: and nothing shall by any means hurt you."

Forgiving people who have hurt you:

"Dear Heavenly Father, I forgive (envision the person's face or say their name). I ask you to cut any ungodly soul ties between myself and (the name of the person), in the name of Jesus."

"I forgive them and release any resentment toward them; and I ask You to forgive me and I now forgive myself in the name of Jesus Christ."

"Dear Lord Jesus, establish in me Your response patterns for this particular category of experience."

Take a moment to turn back to Chapter 2 where I listed statements that affirm who you are in Christ; verbalize those statements with assurance and power. Jesus is love, peace, joy, power, wisdom, and control; therefore, we can claim these things for ourselves with the assurance that we are pouring into our minds great thoughts of victory.

- *The spirit of man is the candle of the Lord, searching all the inward parts of the belly* **(Proverbs 20:27)**.
- *For what man knoweth the things of a man, save the spirit of man which is in him? Even so the things of God knoweth no man, but the Spirit of God* **(1 Corinthians 2:1)**.
- *Therefore judge nothing before the time, until the Lord come, who both will bring to light the hidden things of darkness, and will make manifest the counsels of the hearts: and then shall every man have praise of God* **(1 Corinthians 4:5)**.

Dr. Aiko was instrumental in guiding me into a personal victory. The topic was about the invisible walls that we put up in our life. But this teaching also goes along with those things we put in our mind that can bind us and keep us from victory. Perhaps this personal illustration will be an encouragement to someone who is reading.

I took piano lessons as a child, and as I grew older I became more proficient in learning the classics. When I was about fifteen, I entered a piano competition playing Chopin's *Fantasie Impromptu*, which is a challenging piece, but my teacher believed I could do it so I memorized it in preparation for performing it in competition. In the middle of that performance I got to a point in the music where I drew a total blank. I could not remember a thing! I sat petrified on the bench, but at least I received a good mark and a comment for staying there and maintaining composure. However, I drew a zero for the competition. As a result of that experience, I became absolutely convinced that I could not perform; I was certain that I could not play a piece of music from memory. I believed I was a second rate piano player. Unfortunately, this mindset stayed with me for my entire life (up until the time when I was under the teachings of Dr. Aiko at about age 68 or 69). I quit taking lessons in my sophomore or junior year in high school. Although I played for groups of family and friends and for the church choir, I always had that feeling that I was second best. I am not sure that my piano teacher realized what a deep impact that recital experience had on me, because I probably did not tell her. She wanted me to go on to college and study music, but I lost all desire to do so. Without having a music scholarship I was unable to attend college because my parents did not have the money to cover the cost of tuition, so upon graduating from high school I entered the workforce.

After I became a Christian I felt further failure because I could not play by ear. This was another lie of the enemy, but I believed it too. My heart was always pulled toward the piano, but I started playing the organ for church right after my salvation experience. Generally there wasn't anyone else who could play. I took to the organ easily and played what I called "a happy gospel organ." Since we always sang hymns, it was easy to embellish the music, and blended with the wonderful voices of the choir, the organ and I could make the hymns sound pretty good. Over the years I attended churches that did not have trained music leaders and so I always played in my little comfort zone. I liked to accompany soloists and instrumentalists on the piano, but I never wanted to do solo work. I did not consider the offertories to be anything but part of the service, so I did not feel any intimidation while playing the organ. Also, since I had no desire to be "an accomplished organist," there was no fear of failure when it came to playing the organ. If Handel and Bach could've heard my playing they probably would not have approved of my style. "Too much vibrato!" they would've exclaimed. However, the church folks seemed to like it.

NEVER GIVE UP

When I was in my sixties, I was asked to be the piano accompanist for my church orchestra. I was thinking the director must've made a mistake in selecting me for this position, but I accepted the challenge anyway. Something in me was stirring; I felt that things had to change! Out came the metronome, a lot of practice, and learning a whole new style of contemporary music. I had not practiced like that for years. I enjoyed the rehearsals (sometimes), but concerts or performances brought back that old familiar sense of nervousness and failure like a tidal wave in my mind. I would look at the piano displayed prominently in front of the orchestra and think, *If they would just hide the piano in the back I'd be okay, but here it is, out in front, and here come the nerves!* After retiring, I gave up the piano (again) and thought it was just over. It seemed I had a pattern of giving it up with regularity. I felt too mediocre. I had been the victim of Satan's working on my mind without realizing what had taken place in my young life.

In one of Dr. Aiko's seminars we shared pictures of walls that we envisioned were in our lives. I saw myself at a black piano in an extremely small room that seemed to close in on me. The room was so small that the ceiling was just above my head. It was oppressive. I did see a light that seemed to break through the ceiling. I shared this with Dr. Aiko and told her of some of my experiences with the piano as a young teen. She told me that I had carried the spirit of fear and humiliation regarding my music all through the years. Thankfully, she broke that spirit through prayer.

It took me a little time to realize what had happened, but when I did I began to have confidence in my ability to play the piano, but I had to work to change this mindset that had been a part of me for so long. Change didn't come automatically. The very thought of playing a solo piece before a large audience would cause the fear to come washing over me once again. If I was accompanying a soloist it was different.

I am happy to report the result of conquering this fear (for which I am forever grateful to Dr. Aiko): in my 70th year the Lord laid on my heart to make a piano CD. I picked out the music (this was at the end of January) and practiced. The CD was recorded, produced, and completed by the end of summer. I gave it to my family members at Christmas in 2006 as an inheritance. As I look back I sincerely wish I had practiced longer and harder! This last year, now at age 71, the Lord put a desire in my heart to learn to play by ear via theory, and also to play worship music without written music score in front of me! As I write this chapter, this newfound skill is about to be put into in a performance environment. Is that God or what? For all those years I had carried in my mind that negative impression of myself, and it had caused me to feel failure. I had always assumed that was just simply the way it was, and I never realized it could be different. How wrong I had been! Are you carrying bad memories from negative experiences in your life? If so, please realize that we serve a powerful, awesome God who is the God of second chances and new opportunities. May this testimony I've shared, as well as all that I've written in this book, be an inspiration to you so that you will seek to accomplish your dream!

The great, good news is that the Author of the mind knows what antidotes to give us through prayer, knowledge of the Word, and knowledge of the operation of our brain to break off any bondage that has come to us in any way. The power of the blood of Jesus can be put into effect, and we can change thought patterns through the medicine of the Word and purposefully start to fill our minds with healthy, life-giving thoughts, emotions, prayer, and words that will change the course of our life.

We can rid the toxic waste that has built up in our brains over the years. The feedback loops of our mind can carry the positive and life-giving emotions and thoughts from our brain to create healing within. We can reverse "the curse" and infiltrate our hearts and minds with the positive in a very short period of time. This is so great to know!

It is worth the investment of time and prayer to free your mind and heart of unwanted material. The good news is that you do not have to spend a lot of money in the process. Mainly, trust in the Lord to reveal to you any problem, walls, and barriers in your life that need to come down. He will give you that revelation knowledge and the ability to break those barriers.

The mindset of the flesh is death. The mindset of the spirit is life and peace. The peace Jesus gives means nothing missing and nothing broken: a state of tranquility, harmony, security, safety, and prosperity. Surely that is enough for us to want to guard the thoughts that come into our mind.

Words can captivate thoughts. Positive thoughts can override negative thoughts. In our day when there are so many drugs and medications available to "make us feel better," we must consider the fact that often drugs will suppress the root cause of the problem, which is stress and depression. Of themselves, medications do not cure; they just cover the symptoms.

Fortunately, God Himself puts thoughts into us as well, but they are always thoughts of peace.

Be on guard against what you are thinking.

The following scriptures should be committed to memory so that the Holy Spirit will be able to bring them to your remembrance when you need strength to guard your thoughts. Besides committing scriptures to memory, we must always ask for His help and empowerment, for this is not something we can do on our own.

The Lord has His perfect antidotes:

- *Commit thy works unto the* Lord, *and thy thoughts shall be established* **(Proverbs 16:3).**

Here is another surefire remedy for a great thought life:

- *Finally, brethren, whatsoever things are true, whatsoever things are honest, whatsoever things are just, whatsoever things are pure, whatsoever things are lovely, whatsoever things are of good report; if there be any virtue, and if there be any praise, think on these things. Those things, which ye have both learned, and received, and heard, and seen in me, do: and the God of peace shall be with you **(Philippians 4:8-9)**.*

The following promises are the avenue of peace:

- *Thou wilt keep him in perfect peace, whose mind is stayed on thee: because he trusteth in thee **(Isaiah 26:3)**.*
- *Great peace have they which love thy law: and nothing shall offend them **(Psalm 119:165)**.*

Fear will keep us from trusting the Lord, but **only if we allow fear to come into our mind**:

- *For God hath not given us the spirit of fear; but of power, and of love, and of a sound mind **(2 Timothy 1:7)**.*
- *I thank God through Jesus Christ our Lord. So then with the mind I myself serve the law of God; but with the flesh the law of sin **(Romans 7:25)**.*

Here are a few scriptures with even more promises concerning our mind:

- *For who hath known the mind of **the Lord, that he may instruct him? But we have the mind of Christ (1 Corinthians 2:16)**.*

- *And be renewed in the spirit of your mind (**Ephesians 4:2**).*

There are other wonderful ways to detoxify the brain. I will give you some resources at the end of the chapter.

What is the result of a God-infiltrated mind? Wonderful peace and a mind clear of bad memories and negative thinking. We cannot think two thoughts at the same time. Do you watch over your house and protect it? We need to do the same with our minds.

We cannot be tempted with something that we do not dwell upon. Only think about what you want to come to pass. If you are suffering from any type of addiction, please get a firm hold on this truth. You can tell that habit (**remember:** It first started in the mind) to go and leave you alone in the name of Jesus! You *can* kick a bad habit by changing your thought life as we've discussed in this chapter.

I recently read a startling statistic from AACAP (American Academy of Childhood and Adolescent Psychiatry), which states that children watch three to four hours of TV a day. That comes to 1277 hours a year. The statistics are probably higher among adults. Some people spend several hours every day in front of the TV. Perhaps we should turn from too much TV and instead become a T*hinking* V*entilator* (meaning, the way a ventilator pulls out all the stagnant air and puts in fresh air.)

What could be accomplished in your life if you determined you would give 1277 hours a year or over 3.5 hours a day of your time to a constructive project instead of watching television? You could develop a talent, write a book, set up a business in your home, develop a new and meaningful hobby, take some educational courses—the list is endless. What is it that you want to accomplish in life that is meaningful to you? ... or do you always declare, "I don't have the time!" Analyze where your time is going and what you are doing with your mind.

Are you throwing away three to four precious hours of every day on something that is not giving you a valuable return for your investment of time? As my pastor would say "Selah" – which is written in Psalms at various intervals as a way to convey, "Stop and think on this." Also, consider this: Who and what is putting controlling thoughts into your mind, all because you sit back and let yourself take it in? I can assure you that your idle thinking is being controlled. My friend, I would challenge you to consider this fact. Yesterday's twenty-four hours just flew by and it is impossible to bring them back. You will never have that time again. It is gone. Time is a precious commodity, and we are only given so much in a lifetime. **How are you redeeming your time?**

Dr. Candace Pert is an internationally recognized pharmacologist who has published over 250 scientific articles on peptides and their receptors and the role of these neuronpeptides in the immune system. (She also knows God is the answer.) Dr. Pert reveals that we are biologically "hardwired for bliss and all you need to do is tap into your own body's unlimited natural capacity for living in joy and connecting to the divine." Dr. Pert also stated, "We each have our own inner and natural pharmacy that produces all the drugs we will ever need to run our body/mind in precisely the way it was designed to run. Exogenous drugs (from the outside) are potentially harmful to the system, because they disrupt the natural balance of the feedback loops and influence change at a cellular level."

Let me say this: I am not advocating that you throw out your medications. That can be very dangerous. Consult your doctor. However, I will encourage you to consult Dr. Jesus for His remedies.

I am absolutely and totally convinced that Christians should not be spending time watching secular TV just before going to bed. In fact, I would go so far as to say that a TV set does not belong in the bedroom. Why? Because whatever you saturate your mind with before retiring will do its work while you sleep and will determine how you will start your day when you awaken. Take a moment to think about how you feel when you wake up. We should consider that our day really starts the night before.

Feeding your mind on the Word of God puts life and wisdom into you. It will keep you from sin. You probably know this saying: "**The Bible will keep you from sin or sin will keep you from the Bible.**" Psalm 119:11 declares, *"Thy word have I hid in mine heart, that I might not sin against thee."*

Satan always uses the tactic of bringing doubt and intimidation to the mind. He looks for an opportunity to appeal to our pride. Let's think about the Garden of Eden for a moment. Adam and Eve had everything. They lived in paradise. There was no temptation concerning the misuse of money because they didn't need it. There was no problem with being tempted to commit adultery, because no one else was around. They did not have to keep up with the Joneses because they *were* the Joneses—they had the best of everything. They did not need to go to their closet and deliberate on what to wear for the day! It was a perfect life. In fact, think about how easily the serpent was able to convince them to eat of the forbidden fruit. Why weren't they afraid of the serpent? Could it be that his original purpose in the garden was to watch over the couple for God? Perhaps the devil overheard God give the dominion of the earth to man. He knew he did not have that power and so that is what he went after.

Satan tempted Eve and Adam to doubt God and he appealed to their pride that they could have more. It worked. Why didn't Adam stop the process? They lived in a perfect environment and yet the enemy was able to speak to their minds. Again, the moral of the story is that we need to guard our mind – *always*. Bring in a little doubt and discouragement and soon the negative thoughts will grow.

Satan will bring someone against you to say words that hurt you, and if you are not careful it will began to gnaw at you. When that happens, you probably find yourself thinking lying thoughts such as, *I don't deserve anything;" "How can God use me, look what I've done;" "I can't take this anymore;" "No one loves me; I'm not worth anything;"* Besides the thoughts you'll torment yourself with, you'll also feel bombarded by accusatory thoughts such as, *What makes you think you can do such a thing; You are not qualified; Look how much you have sinned; You are a nobody; You're ugly; You'll never get out of this mess*. It goes on and on. We fall for Satan's lies and then we get into trouble. We begin to mull over the hurts and discouragements in our mind, and soon we find ourselves in doubt or fear. **We need to guard our "self-talk."** As a result of all our negative thoughts and emotions, toxins began to spill out into our body and weaken our immune system.

I can recall times in the past when I allowed negative thoughts to run free. I felt as though someone had thrown a heavy wet blanket over me and I would think, "*I should just quit, I'm not qualified to do this anyway.*" Then, I would snap out of it and think, "*What chapter and verse in the Bible did that come from? None, because it didn't come from God's Word!*" I thank the Lord for Dr. Aiko and others who helped me learn some of these principles and understand the damage we can do to ourselves.

As my pastor very aptly put it in a recent sermon, "Discouragement and doubt automatically affect your dedication. Your dedication will erode." All bad things occur because we did not guard our thought life. Satan can bombard us and we can momentarily go down, but we do not have to stay down. It is not a sin to be hit, but it will become sin if we don't take action to remember who we are, what the Word says, and then dislodge all the attacks.

Wherefore gird up the loins of your mind, be sober, and hope to the end for the grace that is to be brought unto you at the revelation of Jesus Christ **(1 Peter 1:13).**

We can take a lesson from runners competing in the Olympics; they wear the proper gear for running at top speed and they are prepared and focused on the goal. We Christians are like long-distance runners traveling through this world to reach an eternal destination. We are to restrain from those things that distract and hinder us. We must set our minds on reaching the goal of success in Christ and not allow anything to distract us from the goal of obedience. Our minds need to be "girded" up. We need to control our thoughts the same way we control our bodies.

Another guideline for us to follow comes from the following passage:

And be not conformed to this **world***: but be ye* **transformed** *by the* **renewing of your mind***, that ye may prove what is that good, and acceptable, and perfect, will of God* **(Romans 12:2)***.*

Let's take a look at three specific instructions contained within this one short verse.

Instruction #1: The *world's* conduct is not the pattern we should follow.

Instruction #2: We are to be *transformed*: This comes from the same root word that forms the basis of the word *metamorphosis*, meaning a change of form or shape; *transformation* means a change in the form of being (like the transformation of a caterpillar into a butterfly).

Instruction #3: *Renewing of your mind.* When we renew something, it is a complete renovation; a complete change for the better: The meaning of the word *renewing* comes from the Greek word *anakainosis*.

The old, wrong way of thinking must be reshaped, and we can only do this by feeding our minds on the words of the Bible. Then, we are doing the perfect and acceptable will of God. Here comes that word *discipline* again, and *daily*. I personally learned the hard way what happens when I am not in the Word and renewing my mind daily. The mind is prone to "wander." If we are not careful, the enemy sees the loophole and he *will* take advantage. Then we will be saying something or doing something we really did not intend to do.

In contrast, the Word clearly tells us what every Christian needs to do: *"Study to show thyself approved unto God, a workman that needeth not to be ashamed, rightly dividing the word of truth"* **(2 Timothy 2:15).** The word 'study' means "to be eager or earnest to do; to labour, strive, or study." Our eagerness to study the Word and the time we give to it reflects our love for Jesus. Is your heart yearning for answers and truth? Do you want to be lifted from the mundane to live life at its fullest? As you apply the principles presented in the Word you will be absolutely amazed at what you can do.

Pertaining to this discussion of the positive and negative thoughts of the mind, I would like to address the matter of depression. Certainly I do not consider myself an authority, and much has been written to help those who are afflicted. If you are suffering, please seek help. Depression can become most debilitating. However, I believe there are some Christian principles we can apply to our lives as a way to conquer depression: Turn on beautiful Christian music – particularly songs of praise and worship. Open up your Bible and read *aloud* passages from the Psalms that are about thanksgiving, praise, and worship, like Psalm 100. Don't go by your feelings, but begin to thank the Lord for the good things in your life. Go on to praise God for who He is and express your love for Him. Speak out who you are in Jesus. Jesus is an awesome and marvelous Lord and Savior, and He is abundant in mercy and truth. Read Philippians 4:4-10 until your mind has become filled with life. Once you've done these things you will notice the depression has lifted! Why? Because of the positive influence that peaceful thoughts, music, and Scripture have on your spirit, soul, and mind. Scripture, great music, and powerful praises put life into the mind as well as peace.

To obtain victory in your life over whatever is hindering you, quote Scripture prefaced by saying the words "It is written..." Go back to chapter 2 and quote out loud the powerful words of *Who You Are*. Speak to yourself with positive words. Overcome bad thoughts with good thoughts. Overcome the effect of the bad memories by building good ones. Re-channel your thinking. Make a positive commitment that you will forgive all offenses immediately. In that commitment, determine that you will only think and speak healthy thoughts and positive words. Laugh. Get adequate rest and don't allow your body to become exhausted. Learn to love. Think big! Have goals. Work on your dream. When you have accomplished something or the Lord has blessed you in a particular area of your life, write it down. Keep a journal so that later on you can recall past accomplishments and blessings.

- *The preparations of the heart in man, and the answer of the tongue, is from the Lord. All the ways of a man are clean in his own eyes; but the Lord weigheth the spirits. Commit thy works unto the Lord, and* **thy thoughts** *shall be established* **(Proverbs 16:3)**.
- *The Lord will perfect that which concerneth me* **(Psalm 138:8)**.
- *Search me, O God, and know my heart: try me, and know my thoughts: And see if there be any wicked way in me, and lead me in the way everlasting* **(Psalm 139:23-24)**.

Remember that you are designed to succeed. Keep your mind under control so that you don't dwell on past or present hurts, failures, and problems. Keep the lines of forgiveness open between you and others. God supplies the ability and grace to help us change, but we must determine to do the work of bringing about that change. We need to have an **attitude of gratitude** as we continually look forward to blessings and activities. As you apply these principles, it won't be long before you will be walking with a new frame of mind. You will be **P**roductive, **P**leasant, **P**rayerful, and **P**eaceful — *plus* you will *NEVER GIVE UP.*

REVIEW

- Why is it so important to guard our thoughts?
- 87 – 92 percent of all illness starts in the mind.
- We need to be quick to forgive.
- Why must we be careful of perceptions?
- Our time needs to be captured for success. Wasted time cannot be reclaimed.
- We can rebuild our memories from negative to positive, and in doing so, be restored. Can you name one way you can rebuild your negative memories?
- Write down some antidotes for depression and discouragement.
- What portions of Scripture mentioned in this chapter spoke to your heart? Remember to write them down so that you can refer to them later and be encouraged anew once again.

As we move forward from our study of the mind to three of our powerful senses – seeing, hearing, and speaking – we will learn the importance of controlling *the gates* into these senses.

Chapter 4

BE CAREFUL LITTLE EYES

*H*ave you ever seen the figurine of the three little monkeys sitting on a bench? One is covering his eyes, the second is covering his ears, and the third is covering his mouth. Usually the little monkeys had a caption that read, "See no evil, hear no evil, speak no evil." Very wise little monkeys, wouldn't you say?

We will consider the little monkey that is covering his eyes and how that applies to our wonderful eyes. We are so blessed if we have sight. I cannot imagine what it would be like to live in darkness. I love beauty, color, and nature. I enjoy watching people. It is such a blessing to read.

Most little children who have attended Sunday School for any length of time have been taught a wise little song that goes, "Be careful little eyes what you see; Be careful little eyes what you see; For the Father up above is looking down with tender love; So be careful little eyes what you see." The song continues with a verse about the ears and then one about the mouth.

What happens to us as adults? We grow up and seem to feel that our eyes and ears are ours to use for looking at or listening to whatever we desire. Since our eyes are part of our body, we need to give some thought to what we choose to put before them.

God says in His Word, *"The hearing ear, and the seeing eye, the* L*ORD* *hath made even both of them"* **(Proverbs 20:12).**

Sometimes it is the little things that we see that have a great impact on us. When I moved to Texas, a long way from my beautiful mountains, the difference in scenery took a bit of getting used to. I missed the majestic mountains and the tall, stately trees. As the saying goes, "You can take the gal out of the Northwest, but you can't take the Northwest out of the gal." However, I was to learn a great lesson about *looking* at and really *seeing* the beauty around me.

I was in a meeting where the speaker was one who loved wildflowers and photography. He was very knowledgeable in both areas. He liked to scout around Lake Ray Hubbard in North Texas to find wildflowers. Some of these flowers were the size of a thumbnail or even smaller. This photographer would capture their beauty on film, enlarge the pictures, and magnificently display the little creations of God. The tiny flowers were exquisite and absolutely lovely. Man can't make a tree like those in the Northwest and he can't make a gorgeous little wildflower that grows naturally along the banks of a Texas lake, but God can and He did. When we take the time to stop and enjoy our surroundings, no matter where we find ourselves, our visual sense is overwhelmed with the evidence that God has already been there and painted a unique landscape for our enjoyment and blessing. One of the most beautiful sights in the world is that of a little child who is sleeping. We want to capture that moment and keep it forever. Just watching children play can be such a delight. These little moments of "seeing" can bring such a sense of peace. As I am writing it is spring, my favorite time of the year. Every day I go out and look at the progress of the leaves on the trees and see what flowers are coming up in my yard. Yesterday, I put in my begonias and impatiens. I have lined my patio with pots of beautiful geraniums. It is a simple and delightful thing to sit at my kitchen table and gaze at the beautiful flowers as well as watch little birds as they come to get their lunch at the bird feeders.

There is another memorable moment regarding little things that comes to my mind. I was walking down a country road in the Hill Country of South Texas. It was one of those days when the wildflowers were in full bloom. I noticed two little beetles moving a little ball of material. (To us, it could be likened to moving an old, moldy piano.) Now these little creatures do not have the nicest name in the world (dung beetles), nor was the object of their work made from material of our liking, but I was fascinated nonetheless. As they were moving along, one would push while the other would try to keep things in balance. Then they would switch positions. The little beetles worked well together as a powerful team. The distance they covered was amazing considering their size. It made me wonder if we humans would work so diligently and with so much effort when the object of our work was not that appealing. God puts so many little lessons in front of us.

I remember watching an army of ants that were most definitely on a mission. There were hundreds of them filing along in a very orderly line. They knew how to cross the patio and infiltrate the kitchen through a tiny crack. Now their presence was not a welcome sight to me. My mission was to see to it that this ant 'army' was deployed to other parts unknown! However, God says that we should consider the ant. In fact, there is a lesson we can learn from the little things. God does not mince words when He calls someone a sluggard who does not want to work and in contrast He gives the illustration of these industrious little creatures that are always working with such diligence. Isn't it interesting how God uses such **tiny** things in order to teach us **big** lessons?

Here is yet another illustration the Lord gave me. It was one of those gorgeous early summer days. I was on my way to a Christian television station where I worked as a volunteer answering the prayer lines. As I drove I noticed through the car windshield the beautiful, wispy cumulus clouds. In an instant in my mind's eye, I saw a figure that I knew must be likened to Jesus standing in those clouds. In that moment a little song came to me complete with simple words and a catchy tune:

> Jesus is coming again in the clouds of glory,
> Yes, He's coming again in the clouds of glory,
> Jesus is coming again in the clouds of glory,
> What a wonderful marvelous day!

When I go to see my children and grandchildren in Ohio, I sing this little song to the younger ones with a lot of clapping motions. My youngest granddaughter loves this little tune. When I talk to her on the phone from Texas, she often sings it, even after months have gone by since we first sang it together. It is such a simple little tune, but it brings her so much delight. Often when I look up at the billowy clouds, I reflect on the lovely illustration the Lord gave me that day in the form of a little song.

One of my favorite places to visit is an aquarium. What marvelous beauty adorns the fish from the deep. Their gorgeous colors and intricate designs captivate my eyes. The little seahorses are a tremendous and yet delicate work of art. What treasure and sights are in the depths of the seas, yet most of us only occasionally get to see them. What thing of beauty did you pass by today and yet did not take time to reflect on it?

God created our eyes to take in the beauty and glory of His creation PLUS to do so much more. It is time to look into our Bible to learn about the importance of seeing. *"But blessed are your eyes, for they see ..." **(Matthew 13:16)**.*

To see is to *observe closely*. Let us take a look at what Mr. Webster has to say (1828 version) about the word *observe*: "The sense is to hold in view, or to keep the eyes on; to see or behold with some attention." Our heavenly Creator sees all that we do; nothing escapes HIS all-seeing eyes. *"The LORD is in his holy temple, the LORD's throne is in heaven: his eyes behold, his eyelids try, the children of me **(Psalms 11:4)**.* It is a most sobering thought that we are under watch 24/7. There is no place to hide from Him. We may try to put ourselves under a sinful veil of our own doing and pretend that He does not see us, but if we do we are merely deceiving ourselves. *"The eyes of the LORD are in every place, beholding the evil and the good" **(Proverbs 15:3)**.*

It is very good news to those of us who are His children that *"The eyes of the LORD are upon the righteous, and his ears are open unto their cry" **(Psalm 34:15)**.* In the New Testament the Lord makes this contrast: *"For the eyes of the Lord are over the righteous, and his ears are open unto their prayers: but the face of the Lord is against them that do evil" **(1 Peter 3:12)**.*

God gives us an admonition from the Psalmist about what we are to guard our eyes against: *"I will set no wicked thing before mine eyes" **(Psalm 101:3)**.* The same verse in the Amplified Bible reads: *"I will set no base or wicked thing before my eyes. I hate the work of them who turn aside [from the right path]; it shall not grasp hold of me."* When we are told to "let our eyes look straight on," it is for our own good. This is not a judgmental thing; it is a matter of protecting and safeguarding us.

Our eyes are constantly being bombarded by many unwanted visuals. These may come into our field of vision, but we choose whether or not to dwell on the images. If we do dwell on the wrong kind of visual, a picture is taken and transferred to our brain. At a time when we least want to remember it, that picture will come flashing before us. This is one reason why porn is so addictive. We **are** what we watch. It behooves us to be careful. The magazines and books that we read show much about our character. The same is true of TV and movies. Parents, it is imperative to guard the eyes of your children. I will carry this thought even further. If it isn't good enough for children to watch, it probably isn't good for adults either. Just because we are over the age of twenty-one doesn't change the way the eyes and brain work. Visuals are so powerful to our memory. If it is unfit, evil, or ugly, do you really want a permanent photo of it in your mind?

We all know that all media can be used for good or for evil. True success comes in exercising discipline as to what allow into our eye-gate. Success comes in the observation of the little things.

We must guard ourselves even in those things that look good. Remember Eve? First the devil tempted her to doubt God, and then he appealed to her pride. Let's see what happened next. The Bible says Eve **saw** how good the fruit looked! If the enemy cannot tempt us with the evil things, believe me, he will use another means to capture us. Sometimes when things look good it's just a big snare. Certainly Eve set a great precedent for us!

Have you ever purchased something that looked so good at first, but in a short while it turned out to be a problem? Perhaps it was a car or a house. Maybe you were given a great sales job and went by what you saw to be true and thus made an emotional decision. Down the line, the purchase proved to be troublesome. How guilty we are of making purchases without consulting our Source, who is Jesus, about the matter. I've been there and done that in more areas of my life than I care to remember.

I recall when we bought a house that I know was not prayed over. That house was my "thorn in the flesh" for a long time. Finally I decided to make *lemonade from a lemon;* I changed my attitude, did some improvements, and found myself content with my little home. However, I would not be at all surprised when I get to heaven to learn that there was a much better house planned for me if I had only asked God to direct me to it.

The same thing can take place with major life decisions as with purchases. For instance, suppose a job is offered with a raise in pay and perhaps a required move. It looks great and our eyes are on that financial increase. If the decision has not been bathed in prayer, it could cost us more than we can *see.*

It is very possible to have eyes that do not see—spiritually speaking. Our natural eye can see clearly, and yet in the same body our spiritual eye can be blinded because of sin. The natural eye can be full of evil and sin so we cannot see the beauty of the Creator. It is like entering a darkened room while wearing sunglasses. What we take into our eyes illegally (meaning against God's law) comes with a big price tag.

To *see* the good things that are in store for you just lift your eyes upward to the Lord. He is looking down on us watching and waiting with desire and anticipation to bless us, yet our eyes are on everything else. When we lift up our eyes toward Heaven—here comes our help! God will never fail us. We are so busy looking down or looking around at the matter at hand. It is only the upward look that matters.

When I thought I was finished writing this chapter, the Lord showed me such an interesting verse, one that spoke so strongly to me, that I had to come back to this chapter and make some additions. Here is the verse: *"Behold, as the eyes of servants look to the hand of their masters, as the eyes of a maid to the hand of her mistress, so our eyes look to the LORD our God, until He has mercy on us"* **(Psalm 123:2 NKJV)***.* We can be busy with our hands but our eyes are to be looking upward. I will tell you for sure that if our eyes are not in His Word, reading it and meditating upon its great truths **daily**, we will make decisions and mistakes that would never happen if we would let our "eyes wait upon the Lord." He is our strength, our source, and our every present help in time of need. He can save us from a lot of heartache if we allow His Word to *"not depart from our eyes"* and our *"eyes look right... and eyelids look straight" **(from Proverbs 4:20-25)**.*

The successful person will not be self-centered but instead will be focused on others. We are told *"Look not every man on his own things, but every man also on the things of others"* **(Philippians 2:4)**. This can be challenging, but it is another one of those things that if God tells us to do it, then He will give us the grace to do it.

There are so many needs all around us, even in this great land of America. People are hurting and people are lost without a Savior. I recall that Mary Crowley, the founder of Home Interiors, said, "Everyone has an invisible sign around their neck saying they want to be loved." Yes, people need to be loved, and they need us to help them as well as to give them words of comfort and hope. We need to proactively look for ways we can help others.

We are told in the Bible to *look* at the fields, for they are white and ready for harvest. This waiting harvest is the multitude of lost souls who do not know Jesus Christ as Lord. We must take the message to them. I love to go knock on doors and talk with people about Jesus or go into the jails to minister. I have been doing it for years and it is always a joy. Admittedly, there are times the flesh balks, but once I get "into the swing of things," the joy comes. There is something about sharing Jesus that is unlike anything else we can do. I have observed over the years that no matter what the size of the church, those who labor in the fields are a small group. Yet each of us is called to do the witnessing because each has an area of influence that no one else has. We are also told in the Bible that when we are faithful to win souls, we are wise.

We are to LOOK **outward** to the needs of others. We are to LOOK **inward** to "check" on our right standing before God and then, most importantly, we are to LOOK **upward** in anticipation of the return of our Lord. Jesus is coming again. It certainly is not a matter of *if,* but when. Although you may have heard it for years, if He came as you are reading these words, would you be ready? What a day that will be! We need to prepare and be watching so that we are not caught empty-handed. The fantastic mansions of the wealthiest people on earth will not hold a candle to our awaiting homes in heaven! I simply do not have the words to describe the glories of it all. I will give you a hint—take a peek into the last two chapters of your Bible.

We need to ask the Lord to enable us to *see* according to His spiritual realm. I am reminded of some of the lyrics in a great old hymn by Clara H. Scott: "Open my eyes, that I may see, glimpses of truth thou hast for me"; Here is another line: "Open my eyes, illumine me, Spirit Divine." What a powerful prayer in music.

A great prayer given by the Apostle Paul is found in Ephesians 1:17-18 and specifically, in verse 18 he tells us to pray so that *"the eyes of your understanding being enlightened; that ye may know what is the hope of his calling, and what the riches of the glory of his inheritance in the saints..."*

In conclusion, what are you beholding? What are you looking for today? One day all of us will see the Lord of lords and King of kings coming in all of His glory: ***"Every eye shall see him" (Revelation 1:7).*** We are also told that EVERY knee will bow and every tongue will confess the Lord Jesus. At that point, it will be too late if you do not know Him as your Savior and Lord. Let's make a commitment *today* to focus our eyes on the things that are eternal.

REVIEW

- Describe to yourself a beautiful scene of God's creation. Keep it in your memory to reflect on it when you need to.
- Remember, we are never beyond the focus of our heavenly Father.
- Why is it important to look for the little things?
- What effects do inappropriate visual images have on children?
- What two things are important for you to look for?
- Continue to write down scriptures we've studied that have spoken to your heart and spirit.

In the next chapter we will look at the second little monkey who covers his ears and hears no evil.

Chapter 5

BE CAREFUL LITTLE EARS

*Blessed are your eyes,
for they see: and your ears, for they hear.
(Matthew 13:16)*

All of God's creation can hear His voice, and all can emit a sound of praise to Him. He created all things to respond to Him in worship and true praise. God made us to be able to hear Him. The Bible tells us that if we do not praise the Lord, the rocks will cry out. How can they cry out without being able to emit a sound that God could hear?

Researchers in the field of quantum physics have discovered that when the atom is split, there is one particle inside the smallest particle (subatomic particle), and that is sound waves. Sound waves are the smallest living substance unseen by the human eye, and they are the center or core of every living thing. However, everything is made of atoms, and thus, every form of matter emits frequencies and vibrations. There is vibration in our washing machines, microwaves, TV's, furniture etc.

Science is catching up with the Bible!

Did you know that healthy ears actually emit sounds? These sounds are usually very soft, but can occasionally be heard by others. Surprisingly, the person whose ear is emitting the sounds rarely hears those sounds! The cause of these sounds is still under debate, but is thought by some to be due to input from the central nervous system. What matters, however, is that God's divine ear is ever listening for our precious words of exaltation. We see this over and over again in the Scriptures. Whether or not God hears our praise is dependant on the condition of our heart.

In Genesis 1:2 we read, *"The earth was without form, and void; and darkness was upon the face of the deep. And the Spirit of God moved upon the face of the waters."*

Let us look at that word 'moved'. The Hebrew word is *rachaph* (or *rakhaf*), which means to *move, shake, hover.*

From a black void of nothingness, the sound of God's voice created frequencies that brought forth created matter having form and shape. All of God's creation hears and knows His voice. Yes, all things have vibration and movement.

Remember the New Testament story of the fig tree? It heard the voice of the Savior/Creator and had to obey.

Recently we heard a most unusual thing at our church. Our pastor was given a recording of crickets singing. The sound of the crickets had been recorded, engineered, and slowed down. The result: we heard the singing of the crickets in the most marvelous symphony of heavenly music. It was awesome. What a great, powerful, and creative God we serve!

If we listen carefully, we can detect many of the sounds of nature. Our Lord hears them all. What do the walls of your home hear? If they could speak, what would they tell you they hear? Would they say, "I hear sounds of joy?" or, "I hear sounds of love and laughter." or, "I hear harmony and peace." Or …would the walls sadly declare negative words, bickering, backbiting, arguments, and so on? Would the walls want to peel off their paper to cover their ears from the cursing, foul language, or negativity that can possibly be heard in your home?

Nothing escapes the ears of God. He hears all that we say and think. Therefore, we are to be careful what we hear. *"And he said unto them, Take heed what ye hear: with what measure ye mete, it shall be measured to you: and unto you that hear shall more be given"* ***(Mark 4:24)***.

For nothing is secret, that shall not be made manifest; neither any thing hid, that shall not be known and come abroad ***(Luke 8:17)***.

As I was considering this chapter, I found myself thinking about the fact that God hears everything. I was driving to church and took notice of all the apartments, homes, and businesses on my 15-20 minute commute. I thought of the hundreds of people living along this boulevard. What sounds reach the ears of God? Do we stop and think that our Eternal Creator is subject to things that we would not want Him to hear? How many of those people in the stores and residences really care what is being heard? Then I cried out to God, "Oh Lord, how I want to hear from You! Make the words of my mouth and the meditation of my heart be acceptable to You."

The Word tells us, *"Faith comes by hearing, and hearing by the Word of God"* ***(Romans 10:17)***.

As with our eyes, we cannot always control what comes into our ears from the world, but we can control what we allow to stay in our brain.

Consider this: The type of music you listen to is indicative of how you think and who you are. Yes, there are many styles of music, and all of us have different preferences. But do you consider what kind of music will bring a godly atmosphere to your home? Are the airwaves of your house pouring sounds of the secular world into the ears of little children and adults alike, or are you controlling the atmosphere with the life-changing sounds of Heaven? Beautiful music brings an aura of peace. It is amazing how wonderful Gospel music will quiet the stress and tension that may be felt in the room.

Head-banging metal music brings confusion and chaos along with a few other not so heavenly thoughts. It is said that if rock and dissonant music is played regularly in a flower nursery, the plants will wilt.

The fallen Lucifer was a master musician who now seeks to pervert any of God's beautiful melodies. Unfortunately, music is an instrument he uses for his evil influence. When music does not resolve itself and is droning and loud, it puts a stress on the nervous system. Tranquil music soothes our ears and quiets the soul.

Some years back, I went into a local supermarket and immediately noticed that the music was loud and unpleasant. All I wanted to do was to get what I needed and leave. I shared with the store manager, in a kind way, the "psychology of music," (fast music moves us on and out; slow and quiet music invites us to take time to look around) and how the music playing in his store was affecting me. I also stated there might be others who felt the same way. I could tell he was considering what I was saying. The next time I came into the store, the music was entirely different. I saw the manager again and thanked him. You know what? He thanked me. Maybe he had noticed the increase in dollars in the cash registers as a result of making this small change in the atmosphere of his store.

All of us have enjoyed the ambient sounds of ocean waves lapping; gentle rain; the sounds of forest creatures at night. I have a telephone that is programmed to play such sounds.

I am often told that when you enter my home you sense peace. First of all, the Holy Spirit is welcome there and secondly, I play wonderful music all the time.

I go to bed most nights listening to the soothing sounds of heavenly worship music or to Scripture being read aloud. What a wonderful way to go to sleep. When those are the last sounds we hear before falling asleep they stay with us throughout the night bringing peace to our souls.

What is the atmosphere of your car? I call my car *my mobile tabernacle*. There is a lot of praying going on while I am driving. There is either a teaching CD or music playing constantly. It is so interesting to me that when I get into my car my thoughts become directly focused on the Lord. This happens because the atmosphere has been super-charged with God.

Am I trying to call myself a "super saint?" Not at all; in fact, I've learned the hard way that I need the Lord in everything and every place because without Him, I fail and can do nothing. I would love to be able to reclaim the years I lost due to being ignorant of the truths I am sharing with you. All of us have a natural inclination toward the flesh that wants to rule and reign! We need to be educated on how to change.

Take a moment, dear friend, to think on these things. They can be likened to an avenue of blessings on the road to peace. I would encourage you to put all that you have learned into your heart and mind and decide that today is the first day of the rest of your life.

Before we can understand the Word, we must hear it. *"But he that received seed into the good ground is he that heareth the word, and understandeth it"* ***(Matthew 13:23).***

It is so very important to hear what God says: *And we also [especially] thank God continually for this, that when you received the message of God [which you **heard**] from us, you welcomed it not as the word of [mere] men, but as it truly is, the Word of God, which is effectually at work in you who believe [exercising its superhuman power in those who adhere to and trust in and rely on it **(1 Thessalonians 2:13 AMP).***

Remember the story of Mary and Martha in the New Testament? Mary sat at the feet of Jesus. She looked up to Him and listened to what He said. In the same sense, this is exactly what we are doing "when we open the Word of God and look up to the Lord" – we are to sitting at the Master's feet and hearing what He says to us. We hear what He tells us.

Let's read this portion of scripture from the Amplified Bible: *"And she had a sister named Mary, who seated herself at the Lord's feet and was listening to His teaching ... But the Lord replied to her by saying, Martha, Martha, you are anxious and troubled about many things. There is need of only one or but a few things. Mary has chosen the good portion [that which is to her advantage], which shall not be taken away from her"* **(Luke 10:39, 41-42).**

We must first hear before we can believe. Our faith is activated by what we hear, and that gives us the ability to receive. *"My son, attend to my words; incline thine ear unto my sayings"* **(Proverbs 4:20).**

To know spiritual truths means that we listen **carefully** to all that God tells us: *"He that hath an ear, let him hear what the Spirit saith unto the churches; To him that overcometh will I give to eat of the hidden manna, and will give him a white stone, and in the stone a new name written, which no man knoweth saving he that receiveth it"* **(Revelation 2:17).**

Here is another powerful scripture: *"But that on the good ground are they, which in an honest and good heart, having heard the word, keep it, and bring forth fruit with patience"* **(Luke 8:15).**

Although God's primary source of speaking is through His Word, (please never tire of hearing this truth), He does speak to us in other ways. He will speak into our spirit. If we listen carefully, we will hear His words of direction and wisdom. Think of times in your life when you have heard in your spirit a word of caution or wisdom, and it seemed like it just came to you "out of the blue" concerning a particular matter in your life. This is especially powerful when a scripture comes into your mind and it is just what you need for that moment or situation. My friend, this is the Spirit of the Lord guiding you. He can help us to know what to do and what not to do; what to purchase and what not to purchase;

what direction to take and not to take. The Word is profitable, and the Holy Spirit will speak to you through the Word to teach you things that would be impossible to accomplish on your own.

We are prone to want the dramatic. God speaks through miracles, signs, wonders, and visions that have their source in the supernatural. Always, when this occurs, it is for the benefit of man and for the glory of God. Generally speaking, though, we need to **listen for the still small voice of God** and not always expect to see signs and wonders. Remember Elijah in 1 Kings 19. God didn't speak in the mighty wind, the earthquake, or even in the fire. No, God spoke in a still small voice.

I believe He is speaking to us all the time. The problem is not with God. It is that we are not listening. *"Wherefore, my beloved brethren, let every man be swift to hear, slow to speak, slow to wrath"* **(*James 1:19*)**.

As children of God we have been *"delivered from the power of darkness, and translated into the kingdom of His dear Son"* **(*Colossians 1:13*)**. We were spiritually blind and deaf, but now we can see and hear the magnanimous truths that will change our lives forever. What a marvelous, loving heavenly Father we have—One who is so worthy of all our attention and praise.

Do we want to hear the praises and accolades of men in our lives? Perhaps we believe that we are successful when we reach fame and success, accompanied by the applause of men resounding in our ears. However, the true measure of success is found when we come into the presence of Almighty God. If we have been obedient to Him and allowed Him to speak into our ears and heart, then we will hear Him say, "Well done, good and faithful servant." Therein is true success!

REVIEW

- Why was it stated that science is catching up with the Bible?
- We were created to worship and praise God, our Creator. In doing so, we lift Him up in true reverence.
- God hears all that we say and think. Therefore we are to be careful of what we hear.
- Our faith comes by hearing the Word of God.
- To be truly successful, we need to turn a "deaf ear" to the flattery and accolades of men and tune our ears to the voice of God.

In the next chapter we'll discover that our last little monkey is learning a valuable lesson—that there is a time to "cover the mouth."

Chapter 6

BE CAREFUL LITTLE MOUTH

*Death and life are in the power of the tongue:
And they that love it shall eat the fruit thereof.
(Proverbs 18:21)*

The mighty waves of the sea break over the rocky shoreline in a thunderous crash. A voice of thunder resounds from the heavens. Stately cedar trees break and splinter. Animals come to attention in holy fear. The timid young cow is quick to bring forth the calf. The lightning is greater in sound and beauty than a magnificent meteor display. Such splendor would make our 4th of July displays seem like mere sparklers. The vast expanse of wilderness shakes and trembles. The wind blows through the great forests in a symphony of sound! What is this all about? What does it mean? The psalmist tells us *"It is the **voice of the Lord** who sits upon the flood, restraining and directing the affairs of men by His sovereign power."* He is displaying His authority and awesomeness. In the midst of it, God is saying that He will give His people strength, comfort, blessings, and peace. These are mighty words from a majestic God who is absolutely worthy of our adoration. The voice of the Lord declares His majesty.

The preceding words come from Psalm 29. We will cover the worship aspect of this portion of Scripture in chapter 10, "Melodies of Love." In this chapter, however, what I want to convey is this: When God speaks things happen! The Lord demonstrates power in the strength and supremacy of His spoken Word.

Let us go back to the very beginning. In Genesis chapter 1 we read *"and God said"* ten times as the recounting of creation unfolds. God spoke and uttered commands that brought the universe into being. The heavens, the earth, all creatures, man, and every living thing good for man—all were created instantly by the words of the mouth of our Creator God. How superb and marvelous is His voice. He created Adam and Eve to know His voice, and He gave them the ability to communicate with Him. He has done the same for all of mankind.

God upholds all things by the power of His Word. When God says He is going to do something, it is a positive, definite declaration that He **will** do it.

Here is a mighty promise God has given: *"God is not a man, that he should lie; neither the son of man, that he should repent: hath he said, and shall he not do it? or hath he spoken, and shall he not make it good"* **(Numbers 23:19).**

Out of God's lips He spoke these words to the psalmist: *"My covenant will I not break, nor alter the thing that is gone out of my lips"* **(Psalms 89:34).**

When God speaks, it is with the voice of authority. When God speaks, it is true. When God speaks, it is unchangeable. When God speaks, all creation hears!

When God speaks, we should listen.

Let us consider the very small part of our body called the tongue. James 3:5-6 declares that the tongue is a fire and a **world** of unrighteousness, full of every kind of sin imaginable. When we consider the **world**, we are looking at something quit immense. As we read on, it gets worse.

Angry, hurtful, and prideful words that flow from a person's tongue not only inflame that person, but they also inflame and consume others.

How often we hear of wildfires raging out of control along the beautiful western coastline of our country from Southern California up to the great forests of the Northwest. These fires lay waste to hundreds of acres and are often started by a small match, a cigarette, or a spark from a fire pit that was not thoroughly quenched. Great forests are destroyed in minutes. Thousands of acres of trees and woodland beauty are gone, sometimes forever.

Actually, fires can break out anywhere. All of us have witnessed horrible scenes of apartments, businesses, and homes going up in flames so fast that everything in the fire's deadly path is destroyed.

A home across the street from us burned down quickly as we stood helplessly watching the firemen struggling to put out the furious blaze. Devastation and heartbreak always follow such calamities. This powerful force can take out life or cause horrible maiming as the result of its intense burn.

A few years ago, I felt the impact of flames when my car caught on fire in our garage, destroying both the car and the garage. Praise the Lord it was brought under control before we lost our entire home. God literally gave me beauty for ashes in that situation, for which I am most grateful.

The Word says that our tongues can be like fire that is out of control. We can become victims of living in our own parched, dry land because of ignorance of the power of this little instrument for good or evil. As I write this, I earnestly ask the Lord to give me such a picture of the tongue so that the words from my mouth will build up and help rather than inflict pain and hurt others.

Here is another word picture that will help us to understand the result of harmful words: The hunter puts down the trap and sets it, waiting for his prey to come along and get ensnared by it. Likewise, our negative words are like a trap. Out come words that are hurtful, destructive, or angry, and **SNAP**—we are captured by the trap set against us. *"You are snared with the words of your lips, you are caught by the speech of your mouth"* **(Proverbs 6:2 AMP)**

We have been given so many powerful word pictures from the Bible, our Manual of Life, from which we can learn the lessons of life. James continues to teach about the big influence of the little tongue. Would one go to a water fountain and expect sweet water and bitter water to flow out of it at the same time? Would we go to a fig tree expecting to pluck sweet figs, ripe for eating, and get sour green apples? Absolute not. The point, James says, is that too often out of the same mouth comes blessings and cursing, and he gives the clear admonition that these things *"ought not to be."*

Haven't we all let things fly out of our mouth in the heat of the moment, and then later we are sorry for the hurt we've caused and wish we could retract our words? I'm sure we can all plead guilty to this! Someone wisely said that words out of our mouth are like feathers escaping from a pillow in the wind. It is impossible to get them all back.

Most certainly, death and life *are* in the power of the tongue. We are either blessing others or we are negatively affecting them.

"Behold, they belch out with their mouth: swords are in their lip..." **(Psalm 59:7).** We might be inclined to say the word "belching out" brings a rather disgusting picture. You are right. This not a pretty picture! One Bible commentary (Jamieson, Fausset, Brown) said, "They are as ravening dogs seeking prey and as such, belch **out**—that is, slanders with their impudent barkings."

The words (above) are the lowest insult, the basest abuse. They deal in sarcasm, ridicule, slander, and lies. It is a frightening picture.

We will continue to examine truth in the matter.

"A worthless person, a wicked man, is he who goes about with a perverse (contrary, wayward) mouth" **(Proverbs 6:12 AMP).**

We are told that we **WILL** give an account for every idle word that comes out of our mouth; it is not *maybe* but a sure thing that by our words we will be justified or condemned (Matthew 12:36-37). This is a very sobering thought indeed! How important it is for us to keep ourselves in the position of being forgiven and cleansed by the blood of Jesus continually.

We know God is a God of love, truth, and justice. It is interesting to note that Proverbs chapter 6 mentions some things God hates that involve the mouth. In fact, He considers them an abomination:

- God hates a lying tongue.
- God hates a false witness that speaks lies.
- God hates it when discord is sown among His children.

If God hates something, we should also.

Just as we approach a traffic light trust it to safely give us direction, we need to guard our words and look to God's Word for direction. As we're taught in the book of James, we're to be *"swift to hear but slow to speak."*

Wars start by wrong words being spoken. The divorce courts are full of people who said things they wish they could take back. Many children are devastated by the berating words spoken against them. Families are torn apart by words uttered in haste. People are emotionally crippled by abusive words.

Remember the commandment that we are to honor our parents? *"Whoever curses his father or his mother, His lamp will be put out in deep darkness"* **(Proverbs 20:20).** We are living in a society where there is a loss of respect for parents and those in authority. This ought not to be.

Have you ever played the game of Gossip? The first person whispers a phrase to someone next to him or her, and he or she whispers it to the next one, and so on until the last person has heard the phrase whispered to them. By the time the whispered phrase gets to the end of the circle, there is no similarity in wording with the original phrase. We need to be cautious of what we say, particularly when we're speaking about another person. Reputations are ruined by careless words.

Have you ever said something to someone with no malicious intent, and yet they have misinterpreted your words or your meaning? We can say something to another in complete innocence, and by the time it gets to their ears it is taken out of context. The enemy loves to snatch our words and twist them. He even does it with the Word of God, and so he has no qualms about doing it with your words. For this reason, we need to be very careful of not only the words we speak but also the subtext behind those words that might be perceived erroneously by our listeners.

Eliminate the Negative

- Guard your mouth. **(Proverbs 13:3)**
- Speak no evil **1 Peter 3:10; Psalm 34:13)**
- Don't be rash with your words to disturb, alarm, terrify, or hurry others, or to cause them to have anxiety or fear. **(Ecclesiastes 5:2)**
- Let your words be few. **(Ecclesiastes 5:2)**
- Think before speaking. **(James 1:19)**
- Let your yes simply be yes and your no simply no. **(Matthew 5:37)**
- Refrain from being a busybody and saying things that ought not to be said. **(1 Timothy 5:13)**
- Do not slander. **(Proverbs 10:18)**
- We are not to talk about those things done in darkness (sinful and lewd). **(Ephesians 5:12)**

I believe it is time to look at the remedy for ill-chosen words, and to instead see how our words can be a compelling and great force to change our world. Each of us has a sphere of influence. We can win and help others by the words we choose to come out of our mouths. We have a creative force within and we need to confess God's Word constantly by faith, because remember, *"what is not of faith is sin."*

Do you know that you will never defeat the enemy unless you confess the Word against him? He will not back down by your thoughts! You must speak the Word of God in the name of Jesus and declare boldly and authoritatively that he is defeated—and then he **must** back away. When Jesus and Satan were on the mountain and Satan tried to defeat Jesus, the Savior always quoted *"It is written."* Most assuredly, there was power and force behind those words. Jesus won. Satan lost.

It is the same way with claiming healing, victory, or any other promise. You must speak it into being. We are to *"call those things which are not, as though they were"* **(Romans 4:17b)**. This is accomplished by the faith of our words in action. Each of us has a powerful, creative force within us. In the opening statement of his book, *The Tongue, A Creative Force*, Charles Capps makes this statement: "God's Word that is conceived in your heart, then formed by the tongue, and spoken out of your own mouth, becomes a spiritual force releasing the ability of God within you." What a statement!

Everywhere Jesus went He was giving words of life. His words brought forth salvation, miracles, light, comfort, and healing. He responded to words of faith from believing people. *"Every word of God is pure; He is a shield unto them that put their trust in him"* **(Proverbs 30:5)**.

Peter walked with Jesus and loved Him, but in the very crucial hours of the Lord's agony before His crucifixion, Peter cursed and denied Jesus. This flow of words brought Peter anguish of heart and bitter tears. Yet the very same

Peter, when filled with the power of the Holy Spirit, spoke words of life that brought thousands to salvation in Christ. We are so grateful for the mercy and grace the Lord shows us when we fail. He is always there to pick us up.

We can change our world by our mouth. People are dying and going to an eternal hell because Christians are not declaring the Word of God to them so they can make a decision to become a child of God before they die. They will not be changed unless they hear, and how will they hear unless we open our mouths to share the Gospel with them? Are we speaking into our children's hearts the things of the Lord? Are we praying with our mouths biblical prayers that will bring change and healing? Are we givers of life? If we are, then His life coming forth from our mouth will be like healing waters or a peaceful stream coursing its way through a tranquil valley. This course of communication is a better than an angry thunderstorm of ill-chosen words. The Bible gives us specific directions to keep us out of trouble when it comes to choosing our words.

Accentuate the Positive

- Our conversation should become the Gospel. **(Philippians 1:27)**
- God has given us the tongue of the learned so that we can speak right words in due season to comfort others. **(Isaiah 50:4)**
- Our words are to be pleasant. **(Proverbs 16:24)**
- Our words should be appropriate. **(Proverbs 25:11)**
- A wise man's words will be gracious. **(Ecclesiastes 10:12)**
- We should speak the things of God. **(Psalm 145:11)**
- Let your words be "yes, yes" or "no, no." **(Matthew 5:28)**

- We are to make music with our mouth. (**Ephesians 5:19**)
- We are to pray with our mouth. (**Ephesians 6:18**)
- We have been given a heavenly language unto God. (**1 Corinthians 14:2**)
- We are to speak with love. (**1 Corinthians 13:1**)
- Our speech should always be filled with grace and a dash of salt *when needed*. (**Colossians 4:6**)
- We are to comfort one another with our words. (**1 Thessalonians 4:18**)
- We are to please God with our words. (**1 Thessalonians 2:4**)
- We are to witness to the lost about Jesus. (**Matthew 18:19-20**)

What we say is what we get. I want this phrase to burn deep within to the point that we will look at the words that come out of our mouths with a new and greater understanding. When we speak words such as "I am fat" constantly, the body becomes what the mouth declares. If we say we are "worthless" or "no good," we are setting ourselves up for failure. Negative words can hinder lofty goals. People become sick by their words. Constant negative self-talk puts one into inferiority instead of superiority (in the right sense, meaning knowing who we are as sons and daughters of God). We can turn those thoughts into positive words: "I am going to lose weight and stay slender;" "I will be healthy because Jesus said 'by His stripes I am healed';" "I am a victorious person in Christ;" "I can do all things through Christ." Those of my generation will remember the song written by Johnny Mercer and Harold Arlen titled "Accentuate the Positive," which was sung by Bing Crosby. Listen to the truth in these lyrics: "You've got to accentuate the positive, eliminate the negative, latch onto the affirmative, don't mess with Mister In-between."

There is great power in the words that come from our lips. When we speak the words of God, we are speaking life to the hearer. However, when we speak negatively or with cursing, our tongue is being used to create harm to others and ourselves. Satan delights in the latter; when he hears you speaking that way, he knows he has built an inroad for destruction within you. All of us long for encouraging words. We will receive what we speak to others. What is in our heart comes out of our mouth.

The psalmist tells us that meditating on the Word will cause just the right words to come from our mouths. *"I said, I will take heed to my ways, that I sin not with my tongue: I will keep my mouth with a bridle, while the wicked is before me. I was dumb with silence, I held my peace, even from good; and my sorrow was stirred. My heart was hot within me, while I was musing the fire burned: then spake I with my tongue"* **(Psalm 39:1-3).**

This book of the law shall not depart out of thy mouth; but thou shalt meditate therein day and night, that thou mayest observe to do according to all that is written therein: for then thou shalt make thy way prosperous, and then thou shalt have good success.

Good success comes from what we put into our mind and what we say with our mouth. It is not so easy to complain and grumble when we're filling our minds with the promises of God's Word! Trust me and try it. Well-chosen words are *"...like apples of gold in pictures of silver"* **(Proverbs 25:11).**

Let us make this our constant prayer: *"Set a watch, O LORD, before my mouth; keep the door of my lips* **(Psalm 141:3);** and, *"Let the words of my mouth, and the meditation of my heart, be acceptable in thy sight, O LORD, my strength, and my redeemer"* **(Psalm 19:14).**

REVIEW

- When God speaks, it is with authority and absolute truth, for He is righteous and holy. He is the King of kings and Lord of lords, the Creator of all things.
- Out of our mouths will come either blessing or cursing, and are we in control of which it will be. Find two scripture verses given in this chapter that especially spoke to your heart or challenged you, and write them on note cards so that you can keep them before you frequently.
- We are to speak positive words that originate with positive thoughts.
- We will receive whatever we speak.
- Write down what impressed you the most or perhaps a decision you have made regarding the tongue.

In the next chapter we will look at how the heart/soul is the very essence of our success or failure.

Chapter 7

HOW'S YOUR HEART?

We hear so much about keeping our physical heart healthy. We know that it takes proper nutrition and exercise for our hearts to service us well throughout a long lifetime. Some restaurants even show entrees on the menu with a little heart-shaped design next to them and the words, "This entree is *good* for you," meaning we can go ahead and indulge. There are so many sources available to teach us what to eat and how to keep our hearts healthy and in good physical condition. However, in this chapter we are not considering the physical organ of the body. We will be examining our spiritual hearts and souls.

Just as it takes a healthy heart to maintain energy and vitality in the body, so the heart or soul of a person needs to be spiritually healthy. Many Christians have hurting and dysfunctional spiritual hearts. As the heart is, so is the life of a person, *"for out of it (heart) are the issues of life"* **(Proverbs 4:23).** We will return to this verse later.

There are parallels between the physical heart and the spiritual heart:
A healthy physical heart is essential to life.

A healthy spiritual heart is essential for the Christian life.

The physical heart pumps blood to all parts of the body.
The spiritual heart affects every part of the body.

The blood pumped by the heart provides oxygen and nutrients for the body.
The blood of Jesus guarantees vitality and health to the believer and strengthens our spiritual hearts.

The blood flows through the heart in one direction.
There is only one way to receive a new spiritual heart—through belief in Jesus Christ.

The physical heart pumps with a regular beat.
The spiritual heart now beats to a new pace.

Without the heart, the physical body would die.
Without a new spiritual heart, all would face eternal death.

We learned earlier that each one of us is made up of a body, soul, and spirit. We are made up of a body that houses our soul, and within our soul is our spirit. Our spirits need to be changed by the power of God, and when the Spirit of God comes to live within us on the day of salvation, we become who we were truly meant to be when God formed us in the womb. Everything we say and do comes out of our spiritual heart.

A common reference in Christianity is "soul-winning" or "reaching souls." When we say this we are talking about actually taking the Good News of the Gospel to lost people who have never heard of Jesus Christ or accepted Him as their Savior. Once someone has been presented with the

Gospel, he or she is given the opportunity to receive this wonderful exchange we call salvation. It's interesting to note that this fulfillment of the Great Commission is never referred to as going "heart winning" – probably because it's about their eternal soul being saved. However, our purpose in soul winning is also to help each person have a new spiritual heart and life.

In reality, the soul, which makes up the mind, will, and emotions and includes the conscience, has never been naturally regenerated. The soul is referred to as the flesh. When the Spirit of God enters into the inner man where the fleshly spirit once ruled, God the Holy Spirit enables the transformation of the mind, as well as He helps us control our will and emotions. This is what we call receiving a new heart! It is a spiritual transaction. As Christians, we need to *reckon* ourselves dead unto sin and alive unto God on a daily basis. Our minds are cleansed through the reading of the Word of God and the power we gain from it. The Holy Spirit of God empowers us!

The AWMI Commentary (from Andrew Wommack Ministries International) offers an excellent definition of the heart:

> "The word "heart" is used 821 times in the Bible. The plural is used 112 times, and variations such as heartily, brokenhearted, etc., are used 26 times. There are less than 20 references where the word "heart" is referring to our physical organ that pumps blood. Examples: 2 Samuel. 18:14; 2 Kings 9:24.
>
> The dominant words for heart are (1) in the Old Testament Hebrew, "leb," and (2) in the New Testament Greek, "kardia." Both of these words signify the chief organ of physical life, but as has already been mentioned, they are used mainly to

denote the inward mental and moral makeup of man (1 Samuel 16:7)."

Consider the following attributes that come from the heart:

- Imagination of thought **(Genesis 6:5; 8:21; 1 Chronicles 29:18; Proverbs 6:18)**
- Conscience **(1 Samuel 24:5; Acts 2:37; Romans 2:15; Hebrews 10:22; 1 John 3:20-21)**
- Wisdom and understanding **(1 Kings 3:9,12; 4:29; Proverbs 10:8; 11:29; 14:33; 23:15)**
- Pride **(2 Kings 14:10; 2 Chronicles 26:16;; Proverbs 16:18; 18:12; 28:25; Jeremiah 49:16)**
- Gladness or joy **(Proverbs 15:13,15; Isaiah 65:14; John 16:22; Acts 14:17; Ephesians 5:19)**
- Fear **(1 Samuel 28:5)**
- Mischief **(Psalm 28:3; 140:2; Proverbs 6:14)**
- Broken heart **(Psalm 34:18; 51:17)**
- Iniquity **(Psalm 66:18)**
- The issues of life **(Proverbs 4:23)**
- Subtlety **(Proverbs 7:10)**
- Foolishness **(Proverbs 12:23; 22:15)**
- Sorrow **(Proverbs 15:13; Isaiah 65:14; John 14:1; 16:6; Romans 9:2; 2 Corinthians 2:4)**
- Rebellion **(Jeremiah 5:23)**
- Deceit and wickedness **(Jeremiah 17:9)**
- Pureness **(Matthew 5:8)**
- Sin **(Matthew 15:19; Mark 7:21; Acts 5:3)**
- Faith **(Luke 24:25; Acts 8:37; Romans 10:9-10; 1 Timothy 1:5; Hebrews 10:22)**
- Love **(Mark 12:33; Luke 10:27; Romans 5:5; 1 Timothy 1:5; 1 Peter 1:22)**
- Unbelief **(Mark 11:23; Hebrews 3:12)**
- Desires **(Psalms 37:4; Matthew 5:2)**

Our spirit is definitely *part* of our heart (Romans 2:29; 2 Corinthians 1:22; Galatians. 4:6; Ephesians 3:17; and 1 Peter 3:4), but again, only a part. Sin, iniquity, and unbelief come from the heart but not from the born-again spirit. Hebrews 4:12 suggests that spirit and soul are both part of the heart; hence, the Scriptures admonish us to believe with all our heart (Acts 8:37), have singleness of heart (Colossians 3:22), and tell us our hearts can have two minds or two ways of thinking (James 4:8).

Therefore, the term "heart" can include all of the inner man—spirit, soul, or any portion thereof.

As stated, our mind, will, and emotions did not become perfect when we received Christ, and this is true of the heart as well. If they *did* become perfect in that moment, we would be instantly perfect and our world would be a much better place to live. The Spirit of God within our spirit is perfect, but the rest we must continue to work on throughout our lives. That is, the mind, will, and emotions do not become instantly sanctified, purified, or even *sanitized!*

We are warned about the danger of hardening our hearts. Continual sin will harden the heart and the conscience as well. The hardened heart will open up a door for the enemy to come in and play havoc with the mind.

All Christians know the battle that goes on between the flesh and the spirit. Look at Romans 5 and see that we are justified (as if we never sinned), and we are reconciled to God, all because of what Jesus did on the cross. In Romans 6 we learn that we are not to live in sin. The flesh is to be crucified and we are to be alive in Christ. What comes next in Romans chapter 7? A picture of the struggle that brings defeat to man, The Lord in His mercy, does not leave us there; instead, He gives us the wonderful promises of the "how to" in Chapter 8 of Romans.

From the very beginning, the human race has had spiritual heart problems. Every precious little baby, so cuddly and sweet smelling, is born with a spiritual heart condition. True, the child is protected until the age of accountability, but the sin problem has already been inherited as a congenital spiritual heart problem. *"Behold, I was shapen in iniquity; and in sin did my mother conceive me"* **(Psalm 51:5).** It doesn't seem to get any better, for we are told that our *"heart is desperately wicked: who can know it"* **(Jeremiah 17:9).** We can be surrounded by people who look right, sing right, speak right, act right, praise right, and pray right, and yet they can have a deep spiritual heart problem. Fortunately, this is God's business to rectify.

Everything boils down to a heart problem. If the heart is not right with God, our sinful words and actions will betray us no matter how hard we try to cover them up. Surely, the Bible has the answer for all our problems. God's Word is true when it says, *"out of the abundance of the heart the mouth speaks"* **(Matthew 12:34).**

Of the 821 references to the heart in the Bible, 118 of those references are in Psalms, 81 are in Proverbs, and over 100 are in the New Testament. Truly the condition of our hearts is important to God!

In examining these biblical references to the heart, we will consider the positives to keep our spiritual hearts healthy.

From the Old Testament:

- We are to apply our hearts to understanding.
- Let our hearts keep God's commandments.
- Trust the Lord with all our heart.
- Keep our hearts with diligence, because out of it are the issues of life.
- Have a wise heart so we are not as fools.
- A merry heart does good like a medicine.
- A merry heart is reflected on our countenance.

- A righteous heart (meaning one that is in right standing with God) seeks answers.
- One who is wise in heart is said to be of understanding and discernment.
- One who is wise in heart teaches his mouth and adds learning to his lips.
- We are to keep our heart clean.
- As we think in our heart, so are we.
- One with a wise heart will benefit his friends.

From the New Testament:

- We are to have a pure heart.
- A healthy spiritual heart is gentle and meek.
- A healthy spiritual heart is one of faith.
- A good heart will bring forth good treasure.
- We are to have an honest and good heart.
- A healthy heart is a peaceful heart.
- We are to have hearts of joy and rejoicing.
- Our hearts are to have purpose.
- We obey with our hearts.
- The Word of God should fill our hearts.
- We believe with our heart for salvation.

We are to **keep** *our heart with all diligence for out of it are the issues of life* ***(Proverbs 4:23).*** What does it mean to **keep** our heart? This word from the Hebrew word *natsar* means: *"to watch, guard, preserve, guard from dangers, observe, guard with fidelity, be kept close, and be blockaded."* To say it another way: to keep our hearts with all diligence is to be repentant when we sin. As we read the Word, pray, and praise, we will walk in obedience and thus our hearts will stay pure and clean. When there is life in our hearts, our minds are clear, our conscience is pure, the past is redeemed by the Blood of Jesus, and we have hope and joy in the present and for our future in spite of challenges and difficult circumstances we might face. As we prepare ourselves for eternity, we have peace within and hope for the future. Money can never buy this kind of peace. The most wonderful point to remember is that God will never tell us to do something that He will not also *enable* us to do. Therefore, we can have a pure heart.

Before we close this chapter I would like to address a serious issue that affects the status of our heart, which is that of an **unforgiving spirit.**

One of the greatest enemies to a healthy spiritual heart is a root of bitterness from an unforgiving spirit. Many do not understand the dangers and consequences to us mentally, physically, and spiritually when we do not totally forgive others and ourselves. In essence, we grow a hard heart. We might say we forgive on the surface, but we never go deep enough to give **total** forgiveness to the one who has hurt us.

If an unforgiving spirit is allowed to stay in the heart, bitterness and resentment will take root and grow to such an extent that they will eventually eat away at our ability to forgive. Hurt comes to us by many avenues:
- When you've been hurt and you can't let go of it.
- When trust is broken
- Harsh or hurtful words that are spoken to you
- You were given unfair treatment.
- Through emotional, mental, or physical abuse.
- Through sexual abuse
- Pre-conceived idea about a situation when in reality one did not see the whole picture.
- Incidents that happened long ago stay in the mind like barbs.
- Unsettled disagreements that fester
- Unfair disadvantage in financial matters
- Lies were spoken against you.
- You've taken another's offense personally.

- Bitterness from harm that came to a loved one.
- Bitter against God because of the problems you're facing.
- The person to whom the resentment comes may not even know of the problem.

Abuse victims often blame themselves for the wrong that has been done to them. It is a favorite ploy of the devil to deceive the mind of young children and adults who have suffered such awful offenses. It becomes very difficult for an abused person to forgive themselves as well as others.

Even in these difficult situations we are commanded to forgive. Sometimes the hardest person to forgive is self.

When we allow resentment and bitterness to stay within us, it becomes like a **poison**. The poison never goes away. An unforgiving spirit is the root cause. Bitterness and resentfulness can manifest in the form of judgments, anger, unbelief, sickness, bitter words, negativity, stress, inferiority, timidity, and a hard heart to name a few. The poison must come out or it will infect the entire body.

When a hurting person tries to bury or deny a problem of resentment and bitterness, it will not stay buried. The poison of anger, inferiority, and guilt is still in the heart. If a Christian is holding on to such emotions they may not understand who they really are and the true nature of a loving God. The nature of God never stops loving.

Listen to the words of the Lord: *"And when ye stand praying, forgive, if ye have ought against any: that your Father also which is in heaven may forgive you your trespasses. But if ye do not forgive, neither will your Father which is in heaven forgive your trespasses"* (**Mark 11:25-26**). This is clear command to forgive. If unheeded, it will bring serious consequences.

Even lost people gain by totaling forgiving. Not just on the surface, but deep down into the heart. I can think of situations where a child or loved-one has been killed because a terrible incident of abuse or murder and the perpetrator was put into prison. The trials are long, bringing open wounds. There can be a hotbed of hatred and anger. But when loved ones forgive the perpetrator, liberty comes to their soul, whether or not the offender cares to change. When victims refuse or are unable to forgive, they create a "jail" of their own making. When we forgive those who have wronged us, we are set free even if the perpetrator never asks for our forgiveness. This brings about a wonderful sense of liberation for us. We are then free to love.

Here is one way to know your heart. If you have an unforgiving spirit toward a person, then you'll notice that when their name comes before you, or an incident happens that involves them, you'll experience what I call a "ping." The ping is an instantaneous feeling of resentment or dislike. You don't want to reach out and love them. You find it easy to magnify the other person's faults and bring judgment upon them while being unaware of the ugliness in your own heart. Each one of us knows when we have not truly forgiven and forgotten. This unresolved hurt causes us to respond angrily or negatively. The matter is never settled within our soul, and there is no peace in this area. We rehearse issues over and over in our mind. Often the resentment spills out at a most unlikely time. Every one knows who or what is his or her "ping."

Picture a little gate to the entrance of your mind. When we harbor any hurt, resentment, an unforgiving spirit, and so on, we have allowed that gate to be opened and the deceptions of the devil to enter our mind. He loves to mess with our minds. It can be so subtle that we do not realize the source. Satan knows how important it is to God that we forgive others, and he will do his best to add fuel to the fire of hurt and resentments. We then become deceived about our own need. Everything becomes someone else's fault.

Why is having an unforgiving spirit such a serious problem? Because there was One who had to die because of it. Jesus bore the brutality of all our sins, and every offense was nailed to the cross. Jesus' love was and is unconditional, and His mercy abounds. He was the supreme example of forgiving those who reviled Him, hated Him, and treated Him unjustly. In His love by way of Calvary, He provided a way for us to also forgive and love others. **Therefore, we are without excuse if we do not forgive.**

Good news: Total forgiveness sets us free to enjoy peace, joy, and love. The memory of the hurt may not go away, but it will no longer sting. It does not matter what the other person is, does, or even says, the one who forgives will more easily bounce back from an offense done to him/her when he/she has set the offender free. Yes, the forgiver is totally free. The beauty of it all is that the one who forgives can pray successfully for the one who has been hurtful.

The only way out of the problem of having an unforgiving spirit is for us to repent and forgive the one who has hurt us. **There is no other way.**

When we forgive, a spiritual transaction takes place. God blesses those who seek peace and righteousness, and He does it in a marvelous way. When we ask forgiveness for our own sins, He forgives by the power of His blood and puts it behind Him. The Lord will not bring it up again. Satan will try to pollute your mind over and over again with the incident, and your flesh may want revenge, but the Lord never, ever does these things to you.

If there is an issue you need to settle, settle it before it is too late. The subtle thing about an unforgiving spirit is that it will infect everyone around the one who is holding on to such feelings. It ruins relationships and affects children as well the adults in the home. Unforgiveness is a source for bad decisions as well as emotional imbalances and physical calamities.

Let's take a moment to reflect on these powerful words of edification: *"Let no corrupt communication proceed out of your mouth, but that which is good to the use of edifying, that it may minister grace unto the hearers. And grieve not the holy Spirit of God, whereby ye are sealed unto the day of redemption. Let all bitterness, and wrath, and anger, and clamour, and evil speaking, be put away from you, with all malice: And be ye kind one to another, tenderhearted, forgiving one another, even as God for Christ's sake hath forgiven you"* **(Ephesians 4:29-32).**

Wonderful companion verses to read can be found in **Colossians 3:12-17.**

The following verses are important ones to memorize:

O generation of vipers, how can ye, being evil, speak good things? for out of the abundance of the heart the mouth speaketh. A good man out of the good treasure of the heart bringeth forth good things: and an evil man out of the evil treasure bringeth forth evil things **(Matthew 12:34-35).**

For out of the heart proceed evil thoughts, murders, adulteries, fornications, thefts, false witness, blasphemies **(Matthew 15:19).**

For the word of God is quick, and powerful, and sharper than any two-edged sword, piercing even to the dividing asunder of soul and spirit, and of the joints and marrow, and is a discerner of the thoughts and intents of the heart **(Hebrews 4:12).**

But let it be the hidden man of the heart, in that which is not corruptible, even the ornament of a meek and quiet spirit, which is in the sight of God of great price **(1 Peter 3:4).**

The following song from Psalm 51:10 written by Eddie Espinosa speaks to my heart. I play and sing it often. Perhaps you already know it. If not, I would encourage you to learn it and let it minister to your heart:

> Change my heart, O Lord,
> Make it ever true.
> Change my heart, O Lord.
> May I be like You.
> You are the Potter
> I am the clay,
>
> Mold me and make me
> This is what I pray.
> Change my heart, O Lord
> Make it ever true.
> Change my heart, O Lord.
> May I be like You.

And thou shalt love the Lord thy God with all thy heart, and with all thy soul, and with all thy mind, and with all thy strength **(Mark 12:3).**

REVIEW

- We are to continually and diligently guard our heart.
- The term "heart" can include all of our inner man: spirit, soul, or any portion thereof.
- It is dangerous to allow our heart to harden, because doing so allows the enemy to come in and influence our mind.
- An unforgiving spirit is like cancer to the soul.
- Write down what has spoken to your heart in this chapter.

In the next chapter we will learn how to protect ourselves from the enemy.

Chapter 8

EN GARDE!

En Garde is a French term used in the sport of fencing, which simply means to be on guard or to be ready to protect oneself. To guard is to preserve or secure against attack, injury, or loss; to be cautious and vigilant; to defend against the enemy.

Is your armor on tight? Do you know your authority? Are your "weapons" oiled and ready for use? If not, then let this chapter help you come into a full understanding of your authority as a son or daughter of God, because we are in a battle, my precious friends.

Behold, I give unto you power to tread on serpents and scorpions, and over all the power of the enemy: and nothing shall by any means hurt you **(Luke 10:19).**

Because of Satan's deception and his ability to blind, we tend to think the Christian life is too hard, too difficult, or even impossible to obtain. –And the honest truth is that "in the flesh" it is impossible. Not so in the spirit, however; in fact, the opposite is true. When we follow God's Word and depend totally on Him, we find that it is a marvelous, exciting way to live. It does not mean there will not be challenges, battles to win, and obstacles to overcome. What it does mean is that our dependence is totally on another—the person of the Lord Jesus Christ. However, it is our choice to follow Him, and in order to be fit for battle we must choose to exercise discipline and obedience. Obedience is the key.

One of the first things a soldier learns in boot camp is to obey. The drill sergeant knows that the soldier's life and the life of many others will depend on how well the soldier learns this lesson. The same is true with us. Others are depending on us to lead them. We may be the key to saving them from a life of separation from God.

Let us take a look at our adversary. He comes with many names: the adversary, the devil, Satan, Lucifer, prince of the power of the air, prince of this world, god of this world, the accuser, Apollyon, Beelzebub, murderer, tempter, ruler of darkness, the unclean one, and the wicked one, to name a few. Satan is a murderer! The foregoing names sound like a murderer with many aliases whose face is on the FBI's Most Wanted List tacked to a post office wall! Without a doubt, he is exactly that – a criminal of major proportions

Just where did he come from anyway? God created Lucifer. The Bible says the name of Lucifer means "Light bearer; shining one." Lucifer was the anointed cherub. Anointed means "to be set apart for God's divine purpose; bestowed with God's divine favor; an appointment to a special place or function." He was a marvelous, powerful, created being. He was beautiful and full of the music of heaven. *But*... iniquity was found in him. He became full of pride and wanted to be like God. God had to demote him and take him out of his appointed function. He was cast out of heaven. Although the devil is presently the prince of the power of the air, God is not finished with him. God's promises are true and Satan's doom is sealed.

The Bible tells us in Ezekiel 28 that the devil was in the Garden of Eden. It sounds as though he was probably meant to be a ministering spirit to Adam and Eve. God gives His angels to watch over His children and minister to them. Certainly

Adam and Eve seemed to be familiar with Satan. They did not indicate any fear or aversion to him. Satan undoubtedly was listening in when God told our first parents that they would be given dominion and authority over all the earth. Pride and jealousy welled up within Satan's heart. *He* wanted that dominion and authority. He didn't want to see it handed over so easily to these two newly created beings. Satan set about to deceive. Notice his tactics with Eve. Interestingly enough, Adam stood there and didn't do anything about the devil's evil plan except to succumb to his wiles just as Eve had done. Adam and Eve lost their dominion over the earth through giving in to the temptation of the enemy, and the human race has paid a great price as a result of their downfall ever since. All of us might have fallen prey to Satan's temptation just as easily as Adam and Eve did.

Let's take a look at the "I's" of Satan in Isaiah 14:13-14:

I will ascend into heaven,
I will exalt my throne above the stars of God
I will sit also upon the mount of the congregation,
  in the sides of the north:
I will ascend above the heights of the clouds;
I will be like the most High.

His words are PRIDE PERSONIFIED!

And God said to Lucifer, *"Yet thou shalt be brought down to hell, to the sides of the pit."*

Satan's way is hard! Sin comes with a very high price tag, more than anyone wants to pay. It is Satan's desire to kill, steal, and destroy. Sadly, he is doing a good job on many. He has perverted music. He twists God's Word and steals its seeds before it takes root in good soil. He works on the minds of the human race. But Satan can only deceive and intimidate. He is a counterfeit. We must not be ignorant of his devices.

The adversary is like a lion: *"Be sober, be vigilant; because your adversary the devil, as a roaring lion, walketh about, seeking whom he may devour"* **(1 Peter 5:8).** I see the picture of the Lion crouching, waiting for the prey. The lion knows the prey will be as fresh meat, which motivates it to make the kill. The sin in our life is like that fresh meat. When we allow sin to come in and stay, we are the prey for the lion.

There is a parallel between the former verse and an illustration given in Psalm 10. Here we see the psalmist complaining to God about the wicked one. To him it seemed like God was staying afar off. In reality, it is the wicked ones who are standing away from God. Sin always separates us from fellowship with the Father.

When the enemy captures the hearts of men, pride is always at the helm of the problems. Ungodly persecution can follow pride in a godless heart. We clearly see this today in all the acts of terrorism taking place around the world. Behind it all is pride, hatred of Christianity, and belief in a false religion. Our God is a God of love who always seeks the best welfare for His children.

As we continue to look into the teaching of Psalm 10, we see what comes next as a result of the evil heart and pride. Man boasts and says that he can do whatever he pleases to do. He is not looking to God but to himself for the achievement of his goals. It is pride that casts off and ignores the commandments and judgments of God. The downhill spiral continues with deception, lies, and vanity. The wicked one has a hardened heart, and then out of his mouth comes cursing, deceit, and fraud. The wicked man does not think that God sees or hears what he does. If we think that we are not capable of falling into such a trap, consider Saul before his conversion and also Peter before he was filled with the power of the Holy Spirit on the Day of Pentecost. If we are not watchful, it can happen to us. I am sure that many prisoners behind bars wonder, *how did I get here?* In fact, in ministering to inmates, I have heard this over and over again. Some of the inmates are Christians who stopped going to church and turned their backs on the things of God. They wanted it their way, and the end result was incarceration.

Satan's goal is to crush and destroy. Our status in society makes no difference to the devil. Men, women, boys, and girls—all are targets for the enemy. He wants to ruin everyone. His is motivated by his hatred of God and mankind.

Here is the good news: *"LORD, thou hast heard the desire of the humble: thou wilt prepare their heart, thou wilt cause thine ear to hear: To judge the fatherless and the oppressed, that the man of the earth may no more oppress" (Psalm 10:17-18).* He is an awesome God!

We know that Satan is the enemy of the Christian. His demons seek to aggravate and hinder. He is the prince of the power of the air with a hierarchy at his disposal. He is a great liar and the great deceiver. We know he uses intimidation and guilt. He works on the mind. If you are on a guilt trip, my friend, it is the enemy working against your mind.

We are in a war—a great spiritual war! A good soldier must know his enemy and how he operates; otherwise the soldier will be defeated. You see, the devil really isn't all that smart. He uses the same game plan over and over. We need to learn what his *modus operandi* (M.O.) is.

Here is even more good news: Satan is DEFEATED WITH A CAPITOL "D." One of my favorite Bible teachers says he is a zero with the rim knocked out! The Lord tells us that we overcome him by the blood of the Lamb and the word of our testimony. Demons of hell flee when the name of Jesus Christ of Nazareth is spoken. They cringe at the mention of Jesus' blood.

How ignorant I was for so many years because I did not understand about the power of the Holy Spirit and how we could use the Scriptures against the enemy of our soul. I prayed a lot and was faithful to be in church every time the doors were opened, but the enemy attacked me on a regular basis. I did not know how to withstand and eventually overcome the onslaughts he sent my way. I was ignorant of my authority. But rest assured, we definitely have authority over the enemy (Luke 10:19). We do not have to be like the little rag doll tossed about in the mouth of a puppy. We are victorious!

We have been given the whole armor of God, which is everything we need. We are to keep it on tight, and keep it free from holes so that the enemy can't send his darts through it. Review: Our armor is the belt of truth; the breastplate of righteousness; the sandals of peace; the helmet of salvation; the sword of the Spirit, and the shield of faith plus prayer (Ephesians 6:14-18).

I would like to share an illustration the Lord gave to me regarding the armor of God. In this vision I was very dirty with matted hair, and my dress was torn and tattered. My hands were tied to a metal pole. As I looked over my shoulder I saw a giant ugly man with huge arms and a vicious looking weapon in his hand. He was ready to bring it down on me. I knew that I would never survive under such a blow. In that moment, I felt a blow, but I somehow knew that I was not hurt. I looked down and saw that I had no blood on me. When I looked over my shoulder again, I saw blood running as if it were running off a heavy piece of clear Lucite. As I watched this in puzzlement, I heard a voice coming from a brilliant light. The voice said "I am Jesus, and I took your beating for you. If you call out to me to be saved, I will forgive you of your sins and become the Lord of your life. I responded, "Oh yes, Lord, this is what I need and want. I do ask for forgiveness and I want you to be my Savior and Lord." Suddenly I was standing. I looked down and saw that I had on the most beautiful long, white dress that was tailor-made for me. I realized that I had a most lovely golden belt around my waist. *Yes, this must be the Belt of Truth*, I thought. When I looked more closely at my dress, I saw that I was wearing a gorgeous vest with an intricate scarlet thread sewn throughout the garment. *Ah, This is my breastplate of righteousness.* I looked down at my feet and there was a pair of perfectly fitted shoes, very pretty but also comfortable for walking. *My shoes of peace,* I thought to myself. *There must be a special path for me to walk.* I was aware that something was upon my head, but as I put my hand to my head I did not feel anything. Instinctively, though, I knew my head was protected. I had on my helmet of salvation. In my right hand was a shield. It covered my entire body. However, it was not too heavy to hold, and it was a perfect size for me. Then I noticed in my other hand a sword in the shape of a big book. I knew that I had a lifelong long task to learn its contents and to use it wisely. I had been given my personal armor that would protect me throughout my life. Thank you, sweet Jesus.

We are to put on the Lord Jesus and make no provision for the flesh (Romans 13:14). This could be illustrated by putting a hand into a glove or by wrapping oneself in a cloak. Both of these are wonderful illustrations to put in our mind as we approach the throne of prayer. We can see ourselves totally encased in Jesus as He makes intercession for us. In the spirit, we are seated in heavenly places with Jesus.

Guard yourself. The more you seek God, the more the demons of hell will be sent to harass you. I have good news. Some wise teacher said, demons are only little spoiled brats without any power over you. They are just irksome and must leave in the name of Jesus! It is worth repeating: We have been given authority over the enemy by the name of Jesus Christ of Nazareth and because of His shed blood on Calvary.

There are three notorious brothers that we must be careful to recognize. They are the *"tion"* gang. Sometimes they are very subtle in their approach, but nonetheless they're destructive. These three are: Manipula*tion;* Intimida*tion,* Domin*ion (leaving off the "t")*. I would encourage you to see if you have fallen prey to their wiles!

Satan is counterfeit. Jesus is the *real* thing.

- **The wiles of Satan:** He kills, steals, and destroys. **(John 10:10)**
- *The WAY of Jesus:* Jesus gives abundant life. **(John 10:10)**

- **The wiles of Satan:** He intimidates, discourages, depresses, torments, deceives.
- *The WAY of Jesus:* "We are more than conquerors" *(Romans 8:37).* "I can do all things through Christ which strengtheneth me" *(Philippians 4:13).*

- **The wiles of Satan:** He will condemn you and make you feel guilty.
- *The WAY of Jesus:* "There is therefore now no condemnation to them which are in Christ Jesus, who walk not after the flesh, but after the Spirit" *(Romans 8:1).*

- **The wiles of Satan:** A me-first attitude that continually seeks promotions, success, self-exaltation, and the temptations of sin.
- *The WAY of Jesus:* "Seek ye first the Kingdom of God and his righteousness and all these things shall be added unto you" *(Matthew 6:33).*

- **The wiles of Satan:** Fear and unbelief.
- *The WAY of Jesus: "For God hath not given us the spirit of fear, but of power, and of love, and of a sound mind" (2 Timothy 1:7).*

- *The wiles of Satan:* He operates in darkness and evil.
- *The WAY of Jesus: "God is light and in Him is no darkness at all" (1 John 1:5).*

- **The wiles of Satan:** One of his primary objectives is to keep believers out of the Word so they can't use it against him. *"Then cometh the wicked one and catcheth away that which was sown in his heart" (Matthew 16:20).*
- *The WAY of Jesus: "Study to shew thyself approved unto God, a workman that needeth not to be ashamed, rightly dividing the word of truth" (2 Timothy 2:15). "Trust in the LORD with all thine heart; and lean not unto thine own understanding. In all thy ways acknowledge him, and he shall direct thy paths" (Proverbs 3:5-6).*

- **The wiles of Satan:** He deceives believers to feel that they can do it on their own, and he tempts them to put more faith in their five senses than in God. He manipulates people to use their intellect only, or, on the opposite side of the spectrum, to make decisions and approach life based on their emotions.
- *The WAY of Jesus: "But without faith it is impossible to please him: for he that cometh to God must believe that he is, and that he is a rewarder of them that diligently seek him" (Hebrews 11:6). "Faith comes by hearing and hearing by the Word of God" (Romans 10:17).*

- **The wiles of Satan:** Satan is defeated and his demons are brats.
- *The WAY of Jesus:* *"For this purpose the Son of God was manifested that he might destroy the works of the devil"* **(1 John 3:8 and Colossians 2:14-15).**

- **The wiles of Satan:** Satan likes to make us think he has the authority.
- *The WAY of Jesus:* *"Behold I give unto you power to tread on serpents and scorpions and over all the power of the enemy, and nothing shall by any means hurt you"* **(Luke 10:19).** *"And they overcame him by the blood of the Lamb, and by the word of their testimony; and they loved not their lives unto the death"* **(Revelation 12:1).**

- **The wiles of Satan:** Satan's ultimate destiny is hell.
- *The WAY of Jesus:* Our destiny is an eternal heavenly home in the presence of our Savior—no more death or pain, glorious music, perfect relationships, and marvelous work. Praise the Lord.

Satan attacks the physical body, but Jesus wants us to be healthy and whole: *"I pray God your whole spirit and soul and body be preserved blameless unto the coming of our Lord Jesus Christ"* **(1 Thessalonians 5:23).** Even though these promises were written to the Christians in Thessalonica, they are for us today as well because the Word is living and eternal. *"Who his own self bare our sins in his own body on the tree, that we, being dead to sins, should live unto righteousness: by whose stripes ye were healed"* **(1 Peter 2:24).**

We have nothing to fear because the enemy has been defeated: *"And in nothing terrified by your adversaries: which is to them an evident token of perdition, but to you of salvation, and that of God"* **(Philippians 1:28).**

Here is how that same verse reads in the Amplified version of the Bible: *"And do not [for a moment] be frightened or intimidated in anything by your opponents and adversaries, for such [constancy and fearlessness] will be a clear sign (proof and seal) to them of [their impending] destruction, but [a sure token and evidence] of your deliverance and salvation, and that from God."*

Always remember: **the devil has already lost the battle—and we won!** Praise God from whom all blessings flow!

REVIEW

- Lucifer was anointed with the divine favor of God. He was full of the music of heaven.
- Because of pride and the desire to be like God, Lucifer was cast out of heaven.
- The devil's main purpose is to kill, steal, and destroy.
- The devil's plan of operation includes intimation, manipulation, and deception.
- What part of us does he manipulate to carry out his devious ways?
- How does a Christian have authority over Satan's work?
- Quote two Scriptures that we can declare over the work of the enemy.

In the following chapter we will study the revelation knowledge of the power of the Holy Spirit, who is our supreme teacher.

Chapter 9

PLUG IN TO THE POWER

There are two scriptures that resonate in my mind as we approach the subject of the power of God through the Holy Spirit: *"This is the word of the LORD unto Zerubbabel, saying, Not by might, nor by power, but by my spirit, saith the LORD of hosts"* (**Zechariah 6:4**); and, *"It is the spirit that quickeneth; the flesh profiteth nothing: the words that I speak unto you, they are spirit, and they are life"* (*John 6:63*). These are *keys* to the Christian life. I honestly believe that only through His power do we have the ability to **never give up**.

In the great doxology of our faith, we sing "Praise Father, Son, and Holy Ghost"—the almighty triune God! Yes, praise God from Whom all blessings flow! How we need to recognize the function of each member of the Godhead.

Jesus said He would send us a Comforter, a *parakletos* (in the Greek language), the precious Holy Spirit, after His ascension into heaven. The Holy Spirit is the one who convicts us of sin, righteousness, and judgment. Without His work in the heart of an individual, no one would be saved. He comes to live within the life of a new believer and creates a new person in Christ (2 Corinthians 5:17). Our salvation is sealed by the Holy Spirit (Ephesians 1:14). He becomes our Teacher, Guide, Light, and the One who empowers us to live a victorious life as a Christian. What a wonderful fact to know that He will always be our Comforter no matter what the challenge, heartache, or pain. He brings all good things to our remembrance. He longs for our life to be holy so that we may honor and exalt Jesus. He alone can produce holiness. The Holy Spirit waits for us to invite His presence. As Jesus and the Heavenly Father are one, so is Jesus and the Holy Spirit. Holy Spirit produces love, joy, peace, longsuffering (patience), gentleness, goodness, faith, meekness, and self-control with the life of the believer. Try as hard as we might, we will never be able to do this of ourselves. Holy Spirit is our source of revelation knowledge of the Word of God. He is our enabler and encourager. He is the Spirit of Truth.

There are symbols in the Bible that relate to the Holy Spirit:

- **Oil**: anointing, authority, healing power,
- **Dove**: gentle, faithful, compassion, peace, rest
- **Wind**: creativity, power
- **Light**: enlightenment, revelation
- **Fire**: power for witnessing; tongues of fire, purifies
- **Breath**: brings forth life

Jesus taught the importance of the Holy Spirit.

True worshippers must worship Him in spirit and truth ***(John 4:23-24).***

It is the Spirit that quickeneth; the flesh profiteth nothing: the words that I speak unto you, they are spirit, and they are life ***(John 6:63).***

The Comforter is here and will bring all things to our remembrance,

*But the Comforter, which is the Holy Ghost, whom the Father will send in my name, he shall teach you all things, and bring all things to your remembrance, whatsoever I have said unto you (**John 14:26**).*

We are to hunger and thirst for Him.

*In the last day, that great day of the feast, Jesus stood and cried, saying, If any man thirst, let him come unto me, and drink. He that believeth on me, as the scripture hath said, out of his belly shall flow rivers of living water. (But this spake he of the Spirit, which they that believe on him should receive: for the Holy Ghost was not yet given; because that Jesus was not yet glorified (**John 7:37-39**).*

God would never give us something of the devil.

If ye then, being evil, know how to give good gifts unto your children: how much more shall your heavenly Father give the Holy Spirit to them that ask him? **(Luke 11:13)**

There are two baptisms mentioned in Bible.
These can be found in Matthew 3:11, Luke 3:16, and Acts 1:4-5. They are the water baptism by immersion, which shows our obedience in following Jesus' example of being baptized in water, and it also signifies a new or renewed relationship with Him. The Bible actually commands that we are to be baptized in water.

The second baptism is the Baptism of the Holy Spirit, which is for empowerment to do His will. This second experience occurs when the Holy Spirit of the living God comes upon us and empowers us for His service and glory. It is

His gift to us. After the crucifixion of Jesus and His resurrection from the dead, He came to his disciples who loved Him. They had walked with Him. Scripture says that *"He breathed on them, and said unto them, Receive ye the Holy Ghost" (John 20:22).*

Jesus set the example for us.
Jesus is our source and example for all things. John, who preached repentance and salvation through Jesus, baptized the converts declaring, *"Jesus shall baptize you with the Holy Ghost and with fire" (Luke 3:16).* Jesus set the example of water baptism and also the baptism with the Holy Spirit, which was made evident when the Holy Spirit came upon Him in the physical form of a dove. In this same chapter we learn that Jesus was full of the Holy Spirit when the Spirit led Him into the wilderness; the Holy Spirit prepared Him for the encounter He would have with Satan and his temptations. When Jesus returned after spending forty days in the wilderness, He did so in the power of the Holy Spirit. He gave His own commission in of the following verses in Luke: *"The Spirit of the Lord is upon me, because he hath anointed me to preach the gospel to the poor; he hath sent me to heal the brokenhearted, to preach deliverance to the captives, and recovering of sight to the blind, to set at liberty them that are bruised, To preach the acceptable year of the Lord" (Luke 4:18-19).* This is in fulfillment of prophecy in Isaiah 11:2 and Isaiah 61:1-3. In Luke 4 verse 1, we read that "Jesus being full of the Holy Ghost" was led into the wilderness where He would enter into the temptations of devil. In verse 14, the Word declares that Jesus *"...returned in the power of the Holy Spirit."*

If the perfect Son of God, the Savior of the World, could do nothing of Himself except what the Father told Him, and even Jesus had such a strong empowerment of the Holy Spirit to strengthen Him throughout this temptation experience, how can we possibility not believe in the necessity of the Holy Spirit in our lives or say that we do not need His gift?

Jesus tells His disciples to wait for the Holy Spirit.
They were not to do anything but wait until they were baptized with the Holy Spirit; then they would receive power and the Holy Ghost would come upon them (Acts 1:4, 5, 8).

Then the Day of Pentecost came.
Supernatural power is evidenced in and upon the disciples. First John 2:27 states, *"But the anointing which ye have received of him abideth in you, and ye need not that any man teach you: but as the same anointing teacheth you of all things, and is truth, and is no lie, and even as it hath taught you, ye shall abide in him. And now, little children, abide in him; that, when he shall appear, we may have confidence, and not be ashamed before him at his coming."*

This is a good time to look at distinctive changes that took place in the disciples. What typified their lives before they were baptized with the Holy Spirit? We do know they loved Jesus and walked closely with Him, but we also see them plagued by cowardice, fearfulness, desire for recognition, doubt, weakness, brashness, lack of discipline, and denial. On the Day of Pentecost they received new strength, wisdom, and knowledge, and they were endued with power. They became powerhouses for Christ. We see them preaching with a new level of boldness they had never demonstrated before, with thousands coming to a saving knowledge of Christ. Signs, wonders, and miracles followed them everywhere they went.

The Holy Spirit is received.
Acts 8:12-17 tells how Philip was preaching to the crowds, winning people to Jesus, and baptizing them in

water. When the apostles heard about this, they sent Peter and John to pray for the people and lay hands upon them to receive the Holy Spirit. This demonstrated that the baptism of the Holy Spirit was a separate experience from salvation.

We are familiar with the Damascus Road salvation experience of the apostle Paul as recorded in Acts 9:5-6. Three days later, Ananias came and laid hands on Paul, who was instantly healed and filled with the power of the Holy Spirit. Later, we find Paul speaking to Christians who had already received Jesus and were water baptized yet they knew nothing of the Holy Spirit. Paul laid hands upon them and they too were filled with the power of the Holy Spirit. *"And when Paul had laid his hands upon them, the Holy Ghost came on them; and they spake with tongues, and prophesied" (Acts 19:6).*

How could a murderer and a man greatly feared by Christians become the most prolific writer of the books of the New Testament? By the transforming power of the Holy Spirit of God giving him supernatural revelation.

The Holy Spirit is all truth.

"Howbeit when he, the Spirit of truth, is come, he will guide you into all truth: for he shall not speak of himself; but whatsoever he shall hear, that shall he speak: and he will shew you things to come" (John 16:13).

We are not to quench the Holy Spirit.

"Quench not the Spirit" (1 Thessalonians 5:19). I would like to insert in here that in all my years of being in church I always heard about the Great Commission of Mathew 28:18-20. This is our mandate to reach the lost for Jesus and disciple them in their Christian walk. It was quoted often, but I never heard preaching or teaching on the Great Commission of Mark 16:15-18: *"And he said unto them,*

'*Go ye into all the world, and preach the gospel to every creature. He that believeth and is baptized shall be saved; but he that believeth not shall be damned. And these signs shall follow them that believe; In my name shall they cast out devils; they shall speak with new tongues; They shall take up serpents; and if they drink any deadly thing, it shall not hurt them; they shall lay hands on the sick, and they shall recover.*'" I wondered why.

I can easily see that the commission found in the book of Mark requires something above and beyond our human ability while sharing the Good News. I am not inferring that Matthew 28:18-20 does not require the same power, but Mark 17:15-18 declares the necessity of a special anointing of power for signs, wonders, and miracles. Miracles will not happen without His power and yes, they are happening in the present day on a regular basis. God intends for His children to walk in the supernatural provision of the Holy Spirit. If we are not empowered by the Holy Spirit in our life and in our ministry, neither will be able to withstand the test of fiery trials.

Why do we do what we do? Is it for our own sense of fulfillment? To gain the approval of others? To please those in authority over us so that we might be praised? To gain respect and acceptance? To seek our own honor? Because we feel we have to? We can only honor Jesus as we serve Him through the Spirit.

Jesus saved my soul and filled me with His Holy Spirit.
One day when I was twenty-five and very pregnant with my third child, a Baptist preacher came by my home. He recognized that I did not know Jesus. He led me in prayer "down the Romans Road" into a salvation experience. My experience did not come with "bells and whistles" but immediately I knew that I had changed. I wanted to be in church where the Bible was taught and preached. Previously, it had

not been important to me. From that day to this, I spent all my years in church and church activities. I started to listen to Bible preaching and teaching on the radio during the week. I longed for godliness in my life and in my family. I never wanted the things of this world nor did I not want to take part in anything the world offered. Early on, I learned how to win souls, and "knocking on doors" to share Jesus with others became a regular routine.

In my early Christian experience I thought standards of dress and behavior were a way to holiness. I did not realize the legalism that could be attached to it when we put undue emphasis on the outward appearance. When God's Word is not administered with the love and power of Jesus, legalism and bondage can easily get mixed in. There is a difference between legalism and holiness of the heart. Legalism demands keeping the law and adhering to strict rules, which can produce a seemingly holy outward appearance but which often masks inner rebellion. Only the Holy Spirit can produce holiness. Please do not misunderstand me. I strongly believe that we are to dress modestly and appropriately, and to exemplify good character. God requires separation from the world and holiness of heart, and we are inspired to honor Him in these things out of love and respect for our Savior.

When my husband and I moved to Colorado Springs, we immediately joined a church and became involved in all church activities. In due time, I attended a citywide denominational women's meeting. The keynote speaker was a little gray-haired, retired missionary to China named Miss Bertha Smith. Her countenance captivated me because there seemed to be such a glow around her. When it was announced that she would be holding a conference and all were invited, I determined in my heart to attend, and when the day came, I drove to the nearby town where it was being held. I do not remember what she taught, but I *do* remember, very vividly, that she prayed for me. I believe with all my heart that her prayer came to fruition in my experience with the Holy Spirit. She was teaching on the spirit-filled life, but I somehow missed the essence of the message. At the end of the conference, she gave me a list of books to acquire from the Christian Literature Crusade (great preachers and leaders of the faith authored these books). I still have them in my library. However, even in the reading of these books, I missed what the Lord wanted me to know. Satan was busy stealing "the seed." Consider this scripture: *"When any one heareth the word of the kingdom, and understandeth it not, then cometh the wicked one, and catcheth away that which was sown in his heart. This is he which received seed by the way side"* ***(Matthew 13:19).***

Right after that meeting I had the "rug of life" pulled out from under me. For years afterward I went through challenging and difficult circumstances. I faced opposition. I remember feeling I was getting second best and that I had failed. I loved my church and being involved in different aspects of ministry, but I really did not know how to overcome the circumstances that were in my life, so I merely endured. Unfortunately, there was no one to teach me of this marvelous truth I had come so close to learning at that conference and in those books. However, God heard the prayer of Miss Bertha Smith, and one day He would position me so that I could learn about His marvelous gift of the Holy Spirit and experience His power.

I did not really know 'who I was in Christ' during all those years. I prayed and loved reading the Word. However, I wasn't doing it effectively, and at times I found it hard. I revered my Bible and it was always close to me. I was faithful in weekly soul-winning outreaches. You could always find me in every revival meeting and prayer service. I played the organ or piano in every service of the church. I found joy in tithing and giving offerings to missions. There was a season when I brought hundreds of children to church on buses and sought to win their parents to the Lord. It all sounds like being a good Christian, doesn't it? However, I was sorely lacking. With all the busy activity of doing the "right" things, there was an unfulfilled need within my spirit. I may have looked okay on the outside, but on the inside I felt full of inferiority, and I lacked true, Christ-like, unconditional love for others. I knew something was missing. The things of God were sacred to me, but I did not understand how to obtain them. It seems incredible to me now that I didn't know the gifts available to me even though I was always involved in fundamental Bible-teaching churches.

But the Lord was always there. I look back and see how He protected me and guided me even when I was not aware of His leadership or His significance to me. I simply was ignorant of the truths that could change my life, particularly the work He is capable of doing in the life of every believer.

As time went by, I spent twenty-five years of my life in full-time Christian work, all in the area of Christian education. By now I had been a Christian for over forty years. When I was sixty-five years old, the Lord began telling me to retire, which I did about six months later.

Soon after retirement I had two profound experiences: 1) a herniated back and a pelvis separated from the hip (too much yard work!); 2) a gift of a video from a friend. After my back was healed (another wonderful testimony), I plugged in the video. The result of its content would have a profound effect on my life and would start me on a new direction in my spiritual experience. I soon found myself on a journey that I had never expected. The Lord was going to take me from all of my comfortable places! Jesus set me on a path that was going to lead me to a marvelous experience with Him. My life was going to take on a radical inward change!

My life-changing experience came in the quietness of my home. It was a sacred and holy time. I remember it well, for there had been nothing like it before in my life, and there has never been anything like it since. I really do not have the words to adequately describe the experience, but I felt the presence of the Lord pouring over me like a liquid love. At one moment I was playing the piano, and the next I found myself prostrate on my face before the Lord—singing, praying, and crying. Perhaps the Lord allowed me to have such a profound experience because of all the years of unhappiness that had seemed to plague me, years when I felt as though I was merely *enduring* life and not really living it. Although I knew something had happened to me, I was not entirely sure what it was. I would eventually realize that I had experienced the baptism of the Holy Spirit. The power source of heaven lit up my life within. This Baptist grandma had been ignited by the fire of God and set free. It was an experience that the enemy can never duplicate. I am so thankful for His amazing grace that was extended to me.

After this experience, the Word of God came as an explosion of light into my heart. I longed to read the Word and meditate upon the precious truths found within its pages, and this hunger was unlike anything I'd ever experienced in my Christian life. I would sit down to rea, planning to get through long passages, but I would find so much richness in just one verse that I would have to stop and take in its meaning. Easily an hour or two would pass by in my time with the Lord before I would even begin my regular daily activities. I understood the work of the Lord differently. My daily walk with Jesus became much more real. He is on my heart when I awake in the morning and on my mind upon retiring at night. I would rather spend time with Him than anyone else. I learned how to pray and get results. Before this experience, I did not know of real worship and praise. Now it is incorporated into my very being. I can more easily recognize the enemy and come against him by the Sword of the Spirit. I have witnessed miracles. I began to get assignments that I could never accomplish of my own. His supernatural leadership and power was available. Also, I was to become more aware of that "still small voice" within my spirit speaking to me and guiding me. The Holy Spirit is so good to remind me of things I need to do. He keeps me from making mistakes when I listen to Him.

Am I saying that I have arrived in my Christian experience? Absolutely not! I am still learning; we never outgrow our need to learn.

For a period of time, I wanted to know why I did not come to this place in my Christian walk during those precious years of raising my children and being so involved in ministry. This was of great concern to me. I asked the Lord why I missed such a gift for so long. I heard the gentle, loving voice of the Lord say to me, "What about the Book you cherished so much? It was always there for you to search." I knew that what He said was true. Jesus and the power of the Holy Spirit had always been there, but I had not been diligently seeking Him in His Word. 'Daily Bible Readings' were simply not enough. This is probably one of the reasons that I am writing these words to you now in this book—so you will not have to wait so long to discover the truth.

In this story of my testimony, there is an essential lesson to learn. I spent so many years "in Christian service" when I was either too tired or too busy to develop the most important thing in my life—my relationship with Jesus. Before entering into Christian vocation, my life was marked with heartaches and challenges about which few people knew. My work in the field of Christian education began when we moved to Texas, and it was demanding. Previously, I had been a stay-at-home mom for about seventeen years, and my secretarial days had long been over. On top of the challenging work I faced, I was busy with my large family and caring for my elderly mother who lived with us. I thought I was setting an example to my children, but in reality I was neglecting to impart spirituals truths to them because of my ignorance. Even while we were living in Colorado, I thought that keeping my children in church, working with me in the bus ministry, and sending them to Christian schools and colleges would solve the problems of a dysfunctional home. However, I was overlooking one critical point—they had missed the same thing I had missed.

I assure you that I never want to go back to the powerless life of joyless endurance I experienced for over forty-two years. Both my personal life and my mind have been transformed. As a grandmother, I have experienced renewed strength and energy, physical healings, increased knowledge of the Word, plus an enablement to accomplish things I never could have imagined before. There is such freedom, peace, and joy in walking with the Lord.

I pray and talk to the Lord, not only as a holy God to be respected and feared, but also as my friend. Out of my heart and mouth comes praise and adoration, something that was truly missing within me for many years. God works the impossible through us by His Spirit for the glory and honor of our Lord Jesus Christ. How else could a grandma begin to study and practice music in her seventies and go on to produce a piano CD when she had not played the piano seriously for years? Last year, the Lord gave me two major challenges, one of which was the writing of this book.

Before the baptism of the Holy Spirit, my life was marked with big **D's**—*Defeat, Doubt, and Dryness,* but now it is marked by *Deliverance.* Are any of the big Ds present in your life? Precious friend, stop right now and bow in prayer and asked to be filled with His glorious Spirit; then ask Him to give you revelation knowledge of Him.

Every experience needs to be verified by Scripture for its validity. I presented some Scripture in the beginning of this chapter. The Old Testament gives prophecy in Joel 2:28,

Isaiah 32:15, Isaiah 59, and Ezekiel 39:29 regarding the outpouring of the Holy Spirit.

Although my experience was a mighty one, walking with the Lord is a **continual, daily process** of surrender. It is not always easy. I may stumble and fall, but I know how to get back up and get going! We must constantly deal with our flesh and be on guard against the enemy. A Bible teacher of mine says it this way: "I have not arrived, but I *have* left the gate!" We are in a world that does not like the Christian. In fact, we are some of the most hated people on earth. Although we are not of this world, we are to live the heavenly life during our earthly journey as a way of preparing ourselves for eternity.

The spirit-filled life is not a life of ease, floating around on a cloud of serenity. Rather, it is one of facing the enemy on the battlefield of life, knowing how to take the Sword of the Spirit, the Word of God, to conquer every enemy that comes against us. It is seeking after holiness. It is learning to pray the Word over requests and needs that come before us. It is hating sin, but loving people. It is totally trusting the Lord for all things. It is faith in action. It is work, but a blessed work.

Is this spirit-filled life challenged? As I said, everything in the flesh wants its own way: where *I* go, what *I* do, what *I* wear, what *I* want to put in my mouth, what *I* want to think, what pleases *me*. The list is endless. We are born wanting to please ourselves. It is an inheritance we have all received from Adam. However, everything of the Spirit wants to please God. This is the reason why the Bible says that the flesh cannot please God. We desire to put the flesh to death, but we find that it is impossible to die to self unless the Lord "does the doing." God speaks to us through our spirit, and He operates through us by way of His Spirit (John 6:33).

Our flesh will always be at war against the spirit. This is such an eternal truth that we might as well settle it, mark it down, and come to fully understand that it is impossible to control our flesh without the power of the Holy Spirit. The flesh always lives in opposition to God. This is why having a complete understanding of Romans chapters 6, 7, and 8 is absolutely essential and pivotal to your transformation from living a "carnal life into the Spirit-filled life." We can never conform to the image of God except by following His way. He abounds in promises and knows the direction we should take. We must *reckon* it and choose God for our self.

We can only please God and worship him through the Spirit. Salvation is free and so are God's gifts, but the spirit-filled life comes with a price. It is called **absolute surrender**. As we continue in our new **power** walk, we must know that Jesus alone supplies our every need. Our faith and trust is in Him. Jesus wants to flows through us until the Living Water spills out to others. The Spirit-filled life is the Lord's desire for **every** Christian.

We must fully grasp and understand that if we choose to live by the flesh, we will flounder and flop around like a fish out of water desperately trying to get air. It is like we are not living in our designated habitat, so to speak.

"For I know that in me [that is, in our flesh] dwelleth no good thing: for to will is present with me; but how to perform that which is good I find not" ***(Romans 7:18).*** Flesh produces the things of the flesh, but the Spirit produces what only God can produce. Tell it to yourself over and over again.

However, I can absolutely assure you that this gift from the Lord will provide you with joy, victory, and abundance, and a mind free of torment and filled with great peace. There is the ever-present awareness that we have a heavenly destination that so outshines this life and every obstacle we face in it. It is worth the price until we arrive in our heavenly home. Most of all, the Holy Spirit gives us the desire to worship and praise the Lord. I played hymns and spiritual songs on the organ and piano for years and never understood the significance of what I was doing. How very sad and ignorant. There is a marked difference in my music today because of the spirit of worship within.

The mighty men and women of the Bible were ordinary flesh and blood just like you and me, but when the extraordinary experience of the living God came upon them they were lifted above the ordinary into the supernatural. (Scripture makes it a point to state that Elijah was an ordinary man just like us!)

From my own perspective, I can see why this truth has been maligned, declared fraud, and misused. Again, who is the author of confusion? It is **always the devil.** The Spirit brings rest and power beyond our human understanding. He allows the supernatural to take place in our lives. God wants to lift us from our own finite understanding and allow Him to accomplish His divine purposes on planet Earth. This relationship to the Lord is such sweetness to our spirit. It is not optional—this precious gift—even though we try to make it so. The work of the Holy Spirit is primary; Jesus provided for it in His supreme sacrifice on the cross.

Here is a very over-simplified illustration to help us understand the source of the needed power within us to be released. The generator (God) is the source; the cables and conduit that have been hooked up from the generator to flow to a main power supply (Jesus). All the power is in place and available, but until the switch is turned on, the power (Holy Spirit) is not ours. We cannot see the power and the energy source around us, but it is there nonetheless. The generator does not turn on the power. The generator is in place. We are in control of the switch. We activate the power through the turning on of the switch. God is always with us. He never leaves or forsakes us. We are the ones who withdraw from Him when we forget that He is our power source.

We need to search the Scriptures and seek the Lord daily. His gift is available for the asking. When the Holy Spirit comes upon a person, there is new wisdom, power, knowledge, love, joy, peace, and godly characteristics. It becomes evident that there is something different in us. Miracles happen. The soul breaks out in worship and praise. Exploits take place that amazes the one in whom they are taking place. Wisdom and strength burst forth like rivers of living waters to bless others and give glory and honor to Creator God. Explosions of creativity take place to such a degree that one cannot imagine it. Dreams comes true and so much more.

If this seems contrary to what you have previously believed or been taught, please be diligent in prayer and in studying the precious Word. Ask the Lord to speak to you. He will settle the matter in your heart. He will illuminate your spirit and soul. You can worship the Lord in spirit and in truth.

Can we say it too often and can we worship Him too much? What a Savior we have in Jesus who took our sins away and provided us an exchanged life and all the benefits of heaven as well as gifts to enjoy on this earth. He takes us out of the mess we make in life and transforms us. I know that I did not deserve anything but hell, yet He gave me everything in abundance. Praise His Name!

During my time with the Lord one morning, the Lord laid the words of a great hymn on my heart, *Without Him (I Can Do Nothing)* by Mylon R. LeFevre, which is based on John 15:5. I was singing this hymn to the Lord. I felt impressed to pick up my pastor Stephen Hill's daily devotion book entitled *Daily Awakenings* and read the devotion for January 16. I glanced across the page and noticed that the previous day's devotion was titled "With the Holy Spirit." What he wrote is so good that it is worth repeating here. It is a wonderful description of how the Holy Spirit ministers to our heart.

"There is such a danger in trying to make it on our own. When we move forward without the guidance of God, we are doomed to failure. The English preacher William Plumer (1802-1880) stated this truth well.

> Our great error is in trying to do without the aid of the Holy Spirit. He is our guide; without Him we err always. He is our light; without Him we are in darkness. He is our strength; without Him we are as weak as water. He is our sanctifier; without Him we are wholly polluted. He applies to us the Word of God for comfort, and for warning, and for cleansing, and for complete salvation. As He garnishes the heavens, so He beautifies the soul and adorns it with the richest graces. To all who receive Him, He is a fountain of joy, life, peace, and purity.
>
> We must remain attached to the vine; the life-giving flow of the Holy Spirit must be continually flowing through our lives. Then, and only then, will the promise come true: "He that abideth in me, and I in him, the same bringeth forth much fruit."
>
> The problem with most Christians is self-reliance. They try to do things on their own. We must heed the words of Jesus, *"I am the vine, ye are the branches: He that abideth in me, and I in him, the same bringeth forth much fruit: for without me ye can do nothing"* ***(John 15:5).***"

Thank you, Pastor Hill, for who you are and how the Lord has used you. Thank you, Holy Spirit. I know that without you I can do nothing!

Recently I was sitting before the fireplace enjoying the fire, watching the flames quietly dancing. My precious friend, we can be like the wood in the fireplace – dead, dry, and ugly, but when the Master strikes the match to the dead wood we become transformed by the fire and produce a beautiful flame, giving light and warmth. We need the match (the igniting) of the Holy Spirit to transform our life.

Oh, the blessings we do *not* have when we do *not* major on the things of the Word of God. All I can say now is "thank you Jesus" for your patience, mercy, and grace, and for loving me all the time. It is never too late to apply the prayer of change. It is never too late for the impossible.

I am convinced that many who carry their Bibles faithfully to church on Sunday are going through the same kind of experience I had. They are defeated in their Christian life without knowing who they really are and without fully understanding the amazing God they serve. Certainly that was true of me!

Satan isn't troubled by church*goers* or Christians who are busy serving on committees and boards; talented choir members or musicians who perform; or those who are involved in every activity of the church—as long as he can keep them ignorant of the promises and power of the Word of God. He knows this knowledge will bring about his demise. He's perfectly content when you sing loud and clap your hands, and tap your feet and say "Amen" on Sunday; but never enter into true praise and worship and relationship with Jesus the rest of the week. The devil goes to great lengths to distract and weaken the church. Satan uses every deceptive device against Christians regarding the truth of being empowered by the Holy Spirit and receiving His Baptism. WHY does he do this? Because he knows it is only through the Holy Spirit that the supernatural will become evident in the life of the believer. It is not plans, programs, or promotions that accomplish the great goals of heaven. I certainly spent enough of my years involved in such activities. *"Who also hath made us able ministers of the new testament; not of the letter, but of the spirit: for the letter killeth, but the spirit giveth life"* ***(2 Corinthians 3:6).***

I would also add that Satan will try to imitate and defraud, but he cannot give you the fruits of the Spirit: love, joy, peace, longsuffering, gentleness, goodness, faith, meekness, and self-control. These are only endued by the Holy Spirit. When these fruits are manifested in our life, it is evidence that the Holy Spirit is working within us.

Also, the Holy Spirit can be grieved. Our denial of Him will cause Him to grieve. When we do not believe in Him with all of our heart, and we do not accept the truth about Him, He grieves. Sin grieves the Holy Spirit. If we do not believe in His supernatural gifts and empowerment in the way He operates, He will withdraw from us. As Christians, He lives within us, but we must meet the conditions of empowerment.

I have often thought *How can we be one in the Spirit as the Bible teaches when we are bound by denominational differences, religious traditions, and many voices all declaring 'we are right'?* We see within the church pet doctrines, doctrinal disputes, judgments against fellow Christians, strife, battles raging, and ever-increasing divisions occurring among the people. Satan must be standing in the wings laughing, because he knows his blinding tactics are working.

It is very clear that we are to be of one body and one spirit. Yes, it is true that we will never exhaust our knowledge of the Scriptures, but God does not put anything in His Word for us that He has not provided a way for it to be obtained. We are one through Him, and the answer is actually simple. Allow the Holy Spirit to have full control of your life. He will always honor Jesus and use His Word. Yes, there can be imbalances in different "Christian camps," and there will always be differences of opinion, but **not** when the Lord is in full control. What a blessing to understand the mystery of godliness, this oneness with Christ. What liberation and what freedom such understanding brings!

The Spirit will guide us and bring us into unity. Could it be that we are more concerned about our denominational preferences and opinions than seeking the voice of the One who is the Way, the Truth, and the Life? Jesus is very logical, simple, and orderly. There is absolutely no division within Him. He is the omniscient, omnipresent, and omnipotent almighty God. There is absolute oneness in the Trinity. This carries us far beyond man's perceptions, traditions, doctrines, and titles.

We do not want to be as those referred to in the list of the wickedness of the last days in 2 Timothy 2:5 – *"Having a form of godliness, but denying the power thereof: from such turn away."* Rather, our goal should be to please the Lord by desiring this admonition in Jude 20-25: *"But ye, beloved, building up yourselves on your most holy faith, praying in the Holy Ghost, Keep yourselves in the love of God, looking for the mercy of our Lord Jesus Christ unto eternal life. And of some have compassion, making a difference: And others save with fear, pulling them out of the fire; hating even the garment spotted by the flesh. Now unto him that is able to keep you from falling, and to present you faultless before the presence of his glory with exceeding joy, To the only wise God our Savior, be glory and majesty, dominion and power, both now and ever."*

Amen!

REVIEW

- Relate in your own words what you have learned from this chapter.
- Why is it essential to have a personal experience with the Holy Spirit to be successful in the Christian life?
- Name two people in the New Testament who were profoundly changed after their experience with the baptism of the Holy Spirit.

- I would encourage you to take a moment to give thanks to the Lord for His wonderful and awesome gifts to us.

Chapter 10

MELODIES OF LOVE

*A*s I was reflecting on the title of this chapter, I looked up the definition of the word *melody* in the original 1828 version of Webster's Dictionary: "an agreeable succession of sounds; a succession of sounds so regulated and modulated as to please the ear. To constitute melody, the sounds must be arranged according to the laws of rhythms, measure, or the due proportion of the movements to each other." Mr. Webster also used this scripture verse to further define *melody*: *"To make melody in the heart, to praise God with a joyful and thankful disposition, ascribing to him the honor due to his name" (Ephesians 5:19-20).* (Wouldn't it be wonderful to have our contemporary dictionaries give Scripture references to word definitions?) What a gift we've been given in the sounds of melody.

I have used this phrase over and over again: "I am presenting nuggets of truth to quicken your appetite for learning more." I think our basket of nuggets is getting full! The truths of this particular chapter can transform you and take you out of the mediocrity of the nominal Christian life into a vibrant relationship with Jesus. When we learn to worship and praise our Creator and Savior with a thankful heart, the heavenly portals of heaven are opened up to us.

To walk with the Lord in a close relationship is to have a melody of love springing from the heart. Our mouth will declare thanksgiving and praise. We must worship our Lord in spirit and in truth; in fact, we are given the commandment to worship and praise Him. We are designed to worship our Creator and God. It is for His pleasure that we are created.

What joy we receive from listening to beautiful music with splendid harmonies. It calms our soul, brings peace to us, causes our hands to clap, and sets our feet to tapping. The melodies that we are addressing are those that bless the Lord as we worship Him and offer our thanksgiving and praise. It must be the sweetest melody of love to His ears. Glorifying God is the melody, and as we worship Him, praise Him, and offer thanksgiving to Him, as well as pray the Scriptures, we are creating a magnificent harmony to the Almighty God of the universe.

What does it mean to glorify God? **Glorify:** 1.To praise, to magnify and honor in worship; to ascribe honor or, in thought or words with due admiration acknowledged. 2. To make glorious; to exalt.

We glorify God by our . . .

- Praise – **Psalm 22:23**
- Prayer – **Philippians 4:6**
- By our entire consecration – **2 Thessalonians 1:12**
- By trusting in His promises – **Romans 4:20**
- Thanking Him – **1 Thessalonians 5:18**
- Dying to self – **John 21:19**
- Confessing Christ – **Philippians 2:11**
- Suffering for Christ – **1 Peter 4:14, 16**
- Surrendering our bodies and spirits to Him – **1 Corinthians 16:20**
- Glorifying Christ – **2 Thessalonians 1:12**
- Bringing forth fruits of righteousness – **Philippians 1:11**

- Faithfulness – **1 Peter 4:11**
- Worship – **John 4:24**
- Songs of praise – **Psalm 33:3**

What is worship? *Shachah* (Hebrew): to fall down, to bow, to reverence; obeisance before God in worship. Webster's 1828 dictionary definition is: to adore; to pay divine honors to; to reverence with supreme respect and veneration; to respect; to honor; to honor with extravagant love and extreme submission.

The following verses contain some wonderful words of worship straight from the Word of God itself:

Thou art worthy, O Lord, to receive glory and honour and power: for thou hast created all things, and for thy pleasure they are and were created **(Revelation 4:11)**.

And I beheld, and I heard the voice of many angels round about the throne and the beasts and the elders: and the number of them was ten thousand times ten thousand, and thousands of thousands; saying with a loud voice, Worthy is the Lamb that was slain to receive power, and riches, and wisdom, and strength, and honour, and glory, and blessing. And every creature which is in heaven, and on the earth, and under the earth, and such as are in the sea, and all that are in them, heard I saying, Blessing, and honour, and glory, and power, be unto him that sitteth upon the throne, and unto the Lamb for ever and ever **(Revelation 5:11-13)**.

Saying, Amen: Blessing, and glory, and wisdom, and thanksgiving, and honour, and power, and might, be unto our God for ever and ever **(Revelation 7:12)**.

And the song of the Lamb, saying, Great and marvellous are thy works, Lord God Almighty; just and true are thy ways, thou King of saints. Who shall not fear thee, O Lord, and glorify thy name? for thou only art holy: for all nations shall come and worship before thee; for thy judgments are made manifest **(Revelation 15:3-4)**.

God is a Spirit: and they that worship him must worship him in spirit and in truth **(John 4:24)**.

The Holy Spirit resides within our spirit. Therefore, worship must come from our spirit It is not determined by our emotions, although it will touch our emotions, but it is an act of our will that the Lord makes real through our spirit because it is He who dwells within us. We choose to exalt our Lord. Worship is based on our relationship to the Lord when we recognize and honor who He is.

Let's take a moment to reflect on Psalm 29:1-2: *"****Give*** *(ascribe glory, come now; provide)* **unto the L**ORD**, O ye mighty, give unto the L**ORD *glory and strength.* **Give unto the L**ORD *the glory due unto his name;* **worship** *the* L*ORD in the beauty of holiness."* God repeats the phrase "give unto the Lord" three times in two verses. If God repeats something three times, He is trying to get the message across. When we study that phrase word by word, we learn that first we are to give ourselves. Then we are to recognize and acknowledge the strength, power, dominion, and awesomeness of His majesty with full adoration to Him and His holiness. Hallelujah to our awesome and mighty Lord (by the way, hallelujah means *Praise to the Lord or Praise Ye the Lord).* The very thought of Him should cause us to sing. For all that He has done for us we can praise Him in return. Our worship is a glorious privilege.

Why worship God? He is our Savior, Creator, Healer, Guide, Protector, Truth, Light, Deliverer, Fortress, Shield, Love, Peace, Advocate, Provider, King of kings, Lord of lords, Soon coming King, Present Help, Grace, Teacher,

Peace, Giver of gifts and abilities, Source of all good things, our Faithful One. God is gracious, full of compassion, slow to anger, of great mercy, and He is good to all. The list is still incomplete!

To get a glimpse of His magnitude, just look into the heavens and gaze at the splendor of His creation. As we marvel at the moon and stars, take in the beauty of a magnificent mountain range, or hear the wind blowing quietly through the trees, we are beholding but a very minute and microscopic portion His creativity. When we turn our focus on all the works that Jesus did for mankind, we are told the "world could not contain all the books that should be written." Jesus gave us **everything** we have that's of any value in life through His sacrifice on Calvary and His redemption of mankind. How can we *not* worship Him?

There is a marvelous passage of scripture in 1 Chronicles 29 that declares the majesty, greatness, creativity, sovereignty, divine ownership, praise, honor, strength, glory and thanksgiving to the name of Almighty God from the mouth of King David, who was a worshipper. It was David's prayer, and he led his people in rejoicing and worshipping the Lord. Worship not only honors God, but the act of it will bless others as well as us. It is as appropriate today as it was then. Worship is eternal: *"Blessed be thou, Lord God of Israel our father, for ever and ever. Thine, O Lord, is the greatness, and the power, and the glory, and the victory, and the majesty: for all that is in the heaven and in the earth is thine; thine is the kingdom, O Lord, and thou art exalted as head above all. Both riches and honour come of thee, and thou reignest over all; and in thine hand is power and might; and in thine hand it is to make great, and to give strength unto all. Now therefore, our God, we thank thee, and praise thy glorious name"* **(1 Chronicles. 29:10-13).**

Praise and Thanksgiving

I heard the most amazing story about praise when I was under the teaching of Dr. Aiko Horman. I mentioned previously that she was an atheist scientist who became born-again, and now she is an incredible and powerful Bible teacher.

We know that the body is an electro-chemical machine. Five scientists headed by Dr. Jerome Stowell developed a measuring device to learn the wavelength of the electrical charges to the brain. This device had a needle that pointed to the center of the scale. On the right (positive) side it was calibrated to 500 points and to the left of center (negative) to 500 points. This same device measured the power used by a 50,000-watt broadcasting station, sending a message around the world, at nine points on the positive side.

The scientists wanted to know what happens in the brain while a person is dying. They chose a lady who was on the verge of death but who was still alert in her mind. They arranged the device in her room—a very tiny microphone by her pillow—so they could hear anything she was saying. In an adjoining room, the scientists were preparing to register the results.

The lady began to pray and praise the Lord. She asked the Lord to show mercy on those who had despitefully used her. She kept affirming her faith in the Lord and declaring how much she loved Him and how He was the living power in her life. She continued in this wonderful adoration and thanksgiving to Her Lord.

The stoic, atheistic scientists had tears flowing down their cheeks, and they were so touched by her praise that they had forgotten to monitor the instrument. They heard the device clicking and looked toward it. In that moment they realized it was at 500 positive and was trying to go higher. In the actual recording of this communication between the dying woman and her God, they learned that it registered fifty-five times more powerful than the 50,000-watt broadcasting station. Praise the Lord!

They decided to record the communication of an angry, mean-spirited man who was using the name of the Lord in vain. In the registering of this experiment, the needle clicked back and forth on the negative side as far as it would go, to 500 points, and the needle was actually trying to go lower. As a result of this experiment, Dr. Stowell became a born-again Christian. I would like to share an excerpt of his words in this article:

> "We had established, by instrumentation, the positive power of God and the negative power of the adversary. We had found that beneficial truth is positive, and that non-beneficial things involving breaking God's commandments are negative in varying degrees.
>
> If we scientists can record these things, I believe with all my heart that the Lord God can keep a record of our thoughts. He has more power than we have, and a better record keeper than any of us on this earth. It is the presence of God in us that gives us power, of whose magnitude we have no conception. I am now a scientist who loves the Lord with all my heart, and mind and soul, and might. I want you to pray for me that I will always think and say and do the things a positive God wants and nothing according to the wishes of a negative adversary who kept me blinded and bound so many years."

Praise is a sure cure for grumbling, complaining, worrying, fretting, and all other negative behaviors. It will keep our tongues undefiled. Praise chases away depression and gloom. It turns mourning into joy. The tongue that is praising God cannot be criticizing others, complaining, or finding fault at the same time. The very act of praise and thanksgiving with a heart of worship takes the focus off of self and onto the One who deserves it. Negativity causes toxic chemicals to be released within us. However, praise releases positive, life-giving chemicals within our mind and body.

It was hard to choose from so many Scriptures, but I encourage you to read the following aloud:

- *By him therefore let us offer the sacrifice of praise to God continually, that is, the fruit of our lips giving thanks to his name* **(Hebrews 13:15)**.
- *Oh that men would praise the LORD for his goodness, and for his wonderful works to the children of men* **(Psalm 107:8)**.
- *And again, Praise the Lord, all ye Gentiles; and laud him, all ye people* **(Romans 15:11)**.
- *I will bless the LORD at all times: his praise shall continually be in my mouth. My soul shall make her boast in the LORD: the humble shall hear thereof, and be glad. O magnify the LORD with me, and let us exalt his name together* **(Psalm 34:1-3)**.
- *Rejoice in the Lord alway: and again I say, Rejoice* **(Philippians 4:4)**.
- *I will declare thy name unto my brethren: in the midst of the congregation will I praise thee"* **(Psalm 22:22)**.

Let us take a closer look at Psalm 100, a very familiar passage of Scripture. *"Make a joyful noise unto the LORD, all ye lands. Serve the LORD with gladness: Come before his presence with singing.* **Know** *ye that the LORD he is God: It is he that hath made us, and not we ourselves; We are his people, and the sheep of his pasture. Enter into his gates with thanksgiving, and into his courts with praise: Be thankful unto him,* *and bless his name. For the* LORD *is good; his mercy is everlasting; His truth endureth to all generations."*

The word "know" in verse three means to *perceive, recognize, understand with approval.* Glorifying the Savior in worship, thanksgiving, and praise is the highest honor we can bestow upon God. We are inviting Him to come and bless us, for we know that He inhabits our praises. He is so worthy. We are His creation, and it is an honor to exalt our Creator. Worship ushers us into the presence of God, and there is nothing more precious than to experience the presence of God through worship. It amazes me that He even provides the actual words, verses, and praise through His Word.

Psalm 100 is really about our relationship to an awesome God. Worship is a major key to the abundant life. *Serve the Lord with gladness*; when the Bible gives us this exhortation, it is not referring to our own manufactured gladness, but that which flows from the spirit within us like rivers of living waters. We are to come into His presence with anticipation, knowing He wants to meet with us. We are to have ever-thankful hearts. We must recognize His greatness. It is about loving God and putting Him first. God is a good God! Jesus did absolutely everything for us. He paid the supreme price.

I guarantee your life will never be the same when you learn the meaning and delight of praising the Savior. Yes, all day long we can give praise and thanks (Romans 12:12). We will know delights that we never dreamed possible when this becomes a part of our everyday routine. My friend, if this has not been your practice, you can start at this moment. Take a moment to pause from reading and reflect on Him.

We see the harmony between the Word of God and praise in the following passages:

- *Let the high praises of God be in their mouth, and a two-edged sword in their hand (**Psalm 149:6**).*

- *Let the word of Christ dwell* [have its home in you] *in you richly in all wisdom; teaching and admonishing* **[training]** *one another in psalms and hymns and spiritual songs, singing with grace in your hearts to the Lord (Colossians 3:16). Let the word [spoken by] Christ (the Messiah) have its home [in your hearts and minds] and dwell in you in [all its] richness, as you teach and admonish and train one another in all insight and intelligence and wisdom [in spiritual things, and as you sing] psalms and hymns and spiritual songs, making melody to God with [His] grace in your hearts" (Colossians 3:16 in the Amplified Version.)*

I cannot say it better than my pastor, Steve Hill, who wrote the following in a Sunday bulletin: "Thanksgiving is appreciation for what God has done. Praise is acknowledging Him for who HE is. Although these two exercises are intertwined, they are distinct in their defining traits. We thank Him with our lips and actions. We articulate words of thanksgiving just as we would with a friend or family member. Then praise begins on the heels of thanksgiving. One of the Hebrew words for praise has to do with "being clamorously foolish; to rave in celebration."

Don't you think God deserves to hear melodies of love to Him from our lips? We are told that if we do not praise Him, the rocks will cry out.

It is worth repeating: When we learn to worship and praise your Creator and Savior and develop a thankful heart, the heavenly portals of Heaven will be opened up to us.

Oh, how many dry years I had! I was totally ignorant of the truth of worshipping and praising Jesus. In the traditional church services I attended throughout most of my life, worship was defined as the singing of hymns or Sunday morning church service. I was thirty-five years into my

Christian life before I was ever in a service where there was genuine praise and worship. It touched my spirit. Still, a few years would pass before I really understood the experience. How pitiful, because I was the one who played the piano and organ to the hymns we sang throughout those years! The enemy subtly works to deceive us of those things that benefit us the most. My life has been changed by this blessed exercise. I cannot say it often enough and strong enough: the act of worship and praise to the Lord transformed my relationship to my Savior later in my Christian life.

Listen to the words of Matthew Henry, which were written more than two hundred years ago: "Let us be much in the exercise of holy joy, and praise. Joy is in the heart of praise, and praise is the language of joy. Let us engage ourselves to these. God has made joy and praise our duty. All the other parts of our duty to God will be pleasant to us when we abound ourselves in joy and praise towards God. Let us not crowd our spiritual joys into a corner of our hearts, nor our thankful praises into a corner of our prayers, Let us live a life of delight in God, and love to think of Him as we do of one whom we love and value."

If you really know that HE IS YOUR GOD, and you understand the wonderful and powerful exchanged life that was given to you at Calvary through the shed blood of the Lamb, then you will delight in singing praises to Him.

In Deuteronomy chapter 28 we are presented with a vivid picture of the blessings and curses of God. Although this passage was directed to the children of Israel and we are now living under the New Testament covenant of grace (and not under the law), the principles still apply to us today. God promised the children of Israel that if they would seek Him diligently, walk in the His ways, and keep His commandments, then blessings would abound. Every aspect of their life would be blessed: their physical health, possessions, family, environment, abundance, favor, status with men, and even the weather. He would overtake their enemies for them. They would be the head and not the tail. However, if they turned from God and did not obey Him and keep His commandments, curses would come that would affect **everything** in their lives, plus they would lose all they had and face serious consequences. The curses were severe. Notice the most important words in verses 47-48: *"Because they did serve the Lord with joyfulness and gladness of heart for the things he did for them, this was instrumental in bringing on the curses even to allowing the enemy to come against them."* He did not refer to what we would call major sins like adultery, murder, drunkenness, and so forth. No, the indictment came from the fact that they **did not praise their heavenly Father** and would not demonstrate a thankful heart.

In the New Testament we are told that we will give account for every idle word we speak. We will be held accountable for the thoughts of our heart as well.

We are told in all of the following verses to praise the Lord in the sanctuary/congregation: ***Psalm 134:2; Lamentations 3:41; 1 Timothy 2:8; Psalm 88:9; Psalm 141:2; Psalm 143).***

Additional Melodies of Love

- *Speaking to yourselves in psalms and hymns and spiritual songs, singing and making melody in your heart to the Lord* **(Ephesians 5:19).**
- *Ye shall have a song, as in the night when a holy solemnity is kept; and gladness of heart, as when one goeth with a pipe to come into the mountain of the* L<small>ORD</small>, *to the mighty One of Israel* **(Isaiah 30:29).**
- *What is it then? I will pray with the spirit, and I will pray with the understanding also: I will sing with the spirit, and I will sing with the understanding also* **(1 Corinthians 14:15).**

In the New Testament letters (epistles) we find the phrase *"grace be with you and peace from God our Father and from the Lord Jesus Christ"* in 1 Corinthians, Philemon, 1 and 2 Peter, 2 John, and Jude. It may be worded slightly differently and in some of those epistles where the word *mercy* is added, but everything we receive from God is by grace, and when we are obedient to him, peace always follows. *"We are Christians (paraphrase) which worship God in the spirit, and rejoice in Christ Jesus, and have no confidence in the flesh"* **(Philippians 3:3).** This is a powerful statement, one that speaks of our walk with the Lord. We are to worship, rejoice, and understand that we cannot put any confidence in our own flesh. Our confidence needs to be completely in Jesus.

The Offering of Thanksgiving

One of the greatest things we can do is to develop an attitude of gratitude. Certainly, this phase is not original with me, but it is a very important attitude of the heart and exercise of the brain. Remember the statement from a previous chapter: "toxic thoughts produce toxic emotions, which produce toxic attitudes, resulting in toxic behavior; 87% to 92% of all illnesses that plague us today are the direct result of our thought life." This means we should take note of our "stinking thinking" and put to practice praise and thanksgiving. Praise will drive the toxic thoughts from our brain and heart. What a bonus! As we please God, we bless our own body and life. Thanksgiving, praise, and worship are so important in our walk with the Lord.

Notice the common denominator of the words *all* or *everything* in the following verses:

- ***In everything*** *(my emphasis) give thanks: for this is the will of God in Christ Jesus concerning you* **(1Thessalonians 5:18).**

- *And whatsoever ye do in word or deed, do **all** in the name of the Lord Jesus, giving thanks to God and the Father by Him **(Colossians 3:17)**.*
- *Giving thanks always for **all things** unto God and the Father in the name of our Lord Jesus Christ **(Ephesians 5:20)**.*

And ... we are to do it ***continually***, as the Word states in Hebrews 13:15.

I often use this exercise in thanking the Lord for who He is and what He has done for me. Perhaps you, too, would like to incorporate this into your devotion. Take the alphabet and give thanks for something according to each letter.

Thank you Lord for . . .

*You are my **A**lpha and Omega, the author and finisher of my faith.*
*You are my **B**right and Morning Star*
*You are my **C**onfidence*
*You are my **D**eliverer*
*You are my **E**verlasting Life*
*You are my **F**aithful Friend*
*You are a **G**reat GOD*
*You are my **H**ealing Jesus*
*You are my **I**ntellect*
*You are my **J**ustifier*
*You are my **K**ind Father*
*You are my **L**ove*
*You are my **M**aster and Lord*
*You are my **N**ever-failing Guide*
*You are my **O**mnipotent Lord*
*You are my **P**rovider*
*You are the **Q**uietness of my soul*
*You are my **R**ighteousness*

You are my Salvation
You are my Truth
You always Understand
You are my Victory
You are my Way
You are the X-ray into my soul
You are my Youth that strengthens me
You are my Zeal

Each time you praise the Lord, the words on the list can change. This is a simple exercise, but it puts our focus on Him.

I regret the years I wasted when I did not realize the importance of all the truths discussed in this chapter. However, I am determined to change that course in my life forever. I have a book entitled *10,000 Things to Praise God For* by Jan Dargatz, which was given to me by one of my children. It is a constant reminder. What a list!!

How long has it been since you not only thanked God for who He is and the wondrous things He has done, but just started thanking Him for people and *things*? Are we thankful for our possessions?

When we become thankful and bless people, it is amazing how our own attitudes change. We can love our enemies!

Often, I will go through my home and begin to be thankful for things I have. I *tell* my car all the time how thankful I am for it. As mentioned earlier, my last car caught fire in our garage, destroying both the car and the garage in 2002. I put in a very descriptive prayer request for another car, down to mileage, warranty, color, price, and leather seats. The Lord gave me just what I asked for. The car is now seven years old and runs beautifully, the best car I have ever owned. I intend to keep it around for many more miles. I don't need a new car every two years. I wonder if it responds to my gratitude? (Remember quantum physics and prayer?) My possessions, household appliances, and clothes in the closet all seem to last longer when I appreciate them. There must be a correlation!

Prayer, the Highest Privilege

I put the subject of prayer under this chapter title because there is nothing more wonderful than singing the beautiful songs of the Psalms to God in prayer. In fact, many scriptures lend themselves to being sung as worship songs. Dick Eastman of the World Literature Crusade made this wonderful comment: "Melody in its truest sense is a gift from God for the purpose of singing praises unto Him. Many Christians, unfortunately, have never learned the beauty of singing a "new" song unto God during prayer. These songs may come straight from the heart with the Holy Spirit creating the melody. Paul spoke of singing "spiritual songs." To sing unto the Lord is to worship God in melody." It is a wonderful source of prayer.

How I love Mr. Webster and his 1828 dictionary! He offers a beautiful definition of prayer: "In worship, a solemn address to the Supreme Being, consisting of adoration, or an expression of our sense of God's glorious perfections, confession of our sins, supplication for mercy and forgiveness, intercession for blessings on others, and thanksgiving, or an expression of gratitude to God for his mercies and benefits."

We can read about prayer, and we can study it and listen to others, but we need to do it! It will become as natural as breathing.

The Preparation, Presentation, and Possession of Prayer

Preparation: To excel in any of our gifts, talents, and abilities, it is important for us to make necessary preparations in order to achieve success. The same is true concerning prayer. I am referring to setting a time every day to meet with the Lord. This will set the entire tone of your day. It will prepare you for all that you will encounter. If it will help, I will share mine.

I have allowed the Lord to usher in my day for some time. I gather an altar of pillows for kneeling with my Bible opened. Usually I have a note pad handy for ideas that might come to mind, or I have my MP3 player nearby, which is programmed with wonderful music. There is a special section for praise and worship music. My hymnbook or a songbook is close at hand. I like to start out by just thanking the Lord for what He has done for me, and then I spend some time in praise and worship before ever petitioning Him in prayer. It is a practice to start with the Psalms or go into verses in Revelation as part of my praise. I always seek cleansing, and I ask the Lord to lead me where I should go in the Word. Also, I have a marvelous book of Scriptures that has been categorized by subject, which I use in my devotion. I read some daily devotion books if time allows. Time flies by. An hour or hour and a half will pass until my elbows tell me it is time to get up! Then in the evening, no matter how tired I am, I spend some time in praise to the Lord.

I would like to tell you that I have done this my entire Christian life, but it would not be true. If I had only known of this wonderful discipline in my early years! Those years were marked with service and rote Bible reading, which did not come close to what the Lord wanted. Praise the Lord for His amazing grace and patience. He never let go of me. He continued patiently with mercy until I grasped the truth He was trying to reveal to me.

I have many books in my library. Although I love books, they cannot and must not take the place of the Word. I desire to be a student of the Word rather than putting the words of man ahead of the treasure found in the Bible.

Whatever you need to do in your schedule, please do not neglect time in devotion. If you have children and loved ones, know that they need what you receive from God during this time as well.

Since we are in a battle against the enemy, we need to prepare our armor each day. Please make sure you thoroughly understand your spiritual armor as described in Ephesians 6:10-19 and that you apply it every day. We already know that a good soldier does not go into battle without his uniform and gear. Neither should we. If your suit of armor is not properly secured each day, the enemy will find a hole and send his fiery dart directly into it. Our armor is secured through prayer. Our minds and hearts must be prepared as well. Otherwise we will be no match for the weakness of our flesh.

Presentation: What a privilege it is to be given the right and authority to enter the throne of grace, and to do so boldly. We can bring all needs, intercessions, supplications, and petitions to the Lord. (See Hebrews 4:4-16.) We can visualize being seated in the heavens, enveloped in Jesus' arms, because He provided it for us *in Ephesians 1:19-23; Ephesians 2:4-6.* Do you realize that because of you position with Him, spiritually, you are above the dominion of Satan and his demons? All are under the feet of Jesus. You have all authority over the enemy through the power of the blood of Jesus! My precious one, it is an unbelievable, awesome privilege to know that we will be met with mercy, kindness, love, and a listening ear at the throne of grace.

Another valuable tool in making preparation for prayer is to learn how to pray the Scriptures. It is the Word that gives life and power—not our praying. Praying with the Holy Spirit brings answers that far surpass our knowledge and ability. The Lord tells us that *"He hastens over His Word to perform it" (Jeremiah 1:12).* His Word does not return void or without affect. He knows where and how to send it as well as how to make it prosper and accomplish His purposes through our prayers *(Isaiah 55:11).*

Holiness is key to a vital prayer life!
Possession: We must take ownership of our prayer. When I first heard a Bible teacher state that God does not answer prayer according to our needs and that He does not respond to our begging, I had to stop and really reflect on that statement. The point the teacher was making was that true prayer comes with absolute trust and faith in Jesus and His Word. Jesus accomplished everything for us at Calvary and set His principles and laws into place. We receive promises when we activate faith in what He has always done. In realty, the faith takes away all the effort in our part and allows us to completely rest in Him. Our faith in God's Word takes the power and transforms it into action.

I know of those who are in pain, stress, trouble, sorrow, grief, or are distraught over a situation they're dealing with, and they become counter-productive when trying to pray because the burden, the problem, or the need has not been given to Jesus first. The ever-present negative emotions are nullifying their prayer. Without realizing it, they are not successful in finding needed relief and victory, because a faith transaction must occur and belief must be in place. I have been guilty of carrying such burdens. Doing so only serves to pull us down physically and mentally.

As we discussed earlier, negative thoughts and emotions send toxic poisons into the body. You can test this. After a confrontation with someone or a stressful experience, you'll notice that your body suddenly becomes tired and your brain is not operating up to par. God made a provision for us to handle the stresses in our life through prayer. Furthermore, prayer is one of the blessings of praise because the mind cannot think two thoughts (both negative and positive) at the same time. Without faith and trust in God's Word, prayer will not get any higher than the ceiling. Faith is God's requirement and His plan. What blessings come when faith and the Word connect!

Also, I cannot emphasize and repeat this enough: Did you know, precious reader, that as a Christian you have all authority over the devil *(1 John 4:4; Philippians 1:28; Luke 10:19)?* You can chop off his plans and ears with the Word and claim every single promise that God gives.

Read, meditate, soak in, and stand on these promises:

- *If ye abide in me, and my words abide in you, ye shall ask what ye will, and it shall be done unto you (**John 15:7**).*
- *Verily, verily, I say unto you, He that believeth on me, the works that I do shall he do also; and greater works than these shall he do; because I go unto my Father. And whatsoever ye shall ask in my name, that will I do, that the Father may be glorified in the Son. If ye shall ask any thing in my name, I will do it (**John 14:12-14**).*
- *And in that day ye shall ask me nothing. Verily, verily, I say unto you, Whatsoever ye shall ask the Father in my name, he will give it you. Hitherto have ye asked nothing in my name: ask, and ye shall receive, that your joy may be full (**John 16:23-24**).*
- *He that spared not his own Son, but delivered him up for us all, how shall he not with him also freely give us all things (**Romans 8:32**).*

What is the key to proclaiming victory in prayer? **The name of Jesus—the name above every name, Jesus Christ of Nazareth, whose Hebrew name is Yeshua, which is sometimes spelled Y'shua.** The name of Jesus is our authority. What a wonderful, beautiful, awesome, mighy name this is: Immanuel (God with us), Jehovah (YHWH)-Jireh, our provider and Bread of Life. The One who quenches our thirst; El Rohi, our Good Shepherd; Jehovah (YHWH)-Rapha, our Healer; Jehovah (YHWH)-Tsidkenu, our Righeousness; El Olam, the beginning and the end; Jehovah (YHWH)-Shalom, our Peace; to name a few. There is no other name under heaven by which we are saved other than His name. The heavenly Father recognizes His Son's name, and for the sake of Jesus' name, He answers prayer that is prayed accordingly to His will. We are not going to God based on any righteousness we have; rather, it is all based on His righteousness. He tells us that our joy can be full through answered prayer because of the name of Jesus. God is a covenant-keeping God.

There are scriptures that I use all the time in my personal time with the Lord. Just this morning I heard the Lord say to me, "Why don't you include them in this chapter?" Praying His Word is the best way to pray. We are so inadequate within ourselves that we can never fail by praying Scriptures—His written Word—back to Him. This is because His Word never returns to Him void. It always accomplishes His purposes and returns the way He sends it. When energized by faith, we know we have the answer—in His way and through His plan.

- *Search me, O God, and know my heart: try me, and know my thoughts: And see if there be any wicked way in me, and lead me in the way everlasting* **(Psalm 139:23-24).**
- *Teach me to do thy will; for thou art my God: thy spirit is good; lead me into the land of uprightness. Quicken me, O Lord, for thy name's sake: for thy righteousness' sake bring my soul out of trouble* **(Psalm 143:10-11)**.
- *Set a watch, O Lord, before my mouth; keep the door of my lips* **(Psalm 141:3)**
- *The Lord is nigh unto all them that call upon him, to all that call upon him in truth. He will fulfil the desire of them that fear him: he also will hear their cry, and will save them* **(Psalm 145:18-19).**

I pray the following prayers over my children and friends constantly:

I cease not to give thanks *for you, making mention of you in my prayers; that the God of our Lord Jesus Christ, the Father of glory, may give unto you the* spirit of wisdom and revelation in the knowledge of him: *The eyes of your understanding being enlightened; that ye may know what is the hope of his calling, and what the riches of the glory of his inheritance in the saints* **(Ephesians 1:16-18)**.

For this cause we also, since the day we heard it, do not cease to pray *for you, and to desire that ye* might be filled with the knowledge of his will in all wisdom and spiritual *understanding; That ye might walk worthy of the Lord unto all* pleasing, being fruitful in every good work, *and* increasing *in the knowledge of God;* strengthened *with all might, according to his glorious power, unto all* patience *and* longsuffering with joyfulness; *Giving thanks unto the Father, which hath made us meet to be partakers of the inheritance of the saints in light* **(Colossians 1:9-12)**.

And this I pray, that your love may abound yet more and more *in knowledge and in all judgment; That ye* may approve things *that are excellent; that ye may be sincere and without offence till the day of Christ;* being filled with the fruits of righteousness, *which are by Jesus Christ,* unto the glory and praise of God **(Philippians 1:9-11)**.

God desires for us to be in prayer for one another continually. Our leaders, pastors, nation, Israel, missionaries, and friends (enemies too) need our prayers as well as our families. When called upon to pray for others, we are always safe in praying the Word on their behalf. We are given this exhortation in Ephesians 6:18. In this particular verse you will find the word *all* mentioned three times—*all prayer, all perseverance, and for all saints*. The reason for this is found in verse 19: to speak the Word boldly, and to make known the mystery of the Gospel.

I want to add that the above is just a sampling. All of His promises are ours. We just need to insert our name into each verse as we read it and claim its promise. Every day He will give you new ones!

God wants **all** to be saved. There is that word again—*all*. It is so important to pray these scriptures over lost loved ones, and when we do, we can be confident that God hears and answers these prayers.

- *The Lord is ... not willing that any should perish, but that all should come to repentance* **(2 Peter 3:9)**.
- *In meekness instructing those that oppose themselves; if God peradventure (May grant) will give them repentance to the acknowledging of the truth; And that they may recover themselves out of the snare of the devil, who are taken captive by him at his will* **(2 Timothy 2:25-26)**.
- *But if our gospel be hid, it is hid to them that are lost: 4In whom the god of this world hath blinded the minds of them which believe not, lest the light of the glorious gospel of Christ, who is the image of God, should shine unto them* **(2 Corinthians 4:3-4)**.

We need to pray against the blindness that the enemy tries to put over our loved ones, and pray the light of the Gospel into their minds and hearts. *"Be careful for nothing; but in every thing by prayer and supplication with thanksgiving let your requests be made known unto God"* **(Philippians 4:6)**. I so desire for these few words on prayer to give you food for thought and to bless your life.

REVIEW

- The sweetest melody of love to the Lord is our thanksgiving, praise, and worship.
- The Word of God is a marvelous praise and worship source.
- Give some examples of how prayer involves preparation, presentation, and possession.
- Holiness is key to a vital prayer life.
- Make note of important Scriptures that spoke to your heart.

Now we will learn how important it is to have energy in our bodies to fulfill the assignments and abilities given to us.

Chapter 11

YOUR MAGNIFICENT MACHINE

*L*et's take a moment to reflect on the powerful words of this portion of Scripture: *"What? Know ye not that your body is the temple of the Holy Ghost which is in you, which ye have of God, and ye are not your own? For ye are bought with a price: therefore glorify God in your body, and in your spirit, which are God's"* **(1 Corinthians 6:19-20).**

If we grasp this marvelous truth, my friend, it will take on an entirely new meaning of how God wants us to take care of ourselves. If we truly are born-again children God, then He is living within each of us through His Holy Spirit. He is dwelling in our temple, which is His tabernacle or holy place. Therefore, your body is the holy dwelling place of the Lord Jesus by His Spirit. What a humbling yet awesome truth! We are designed to be holy, both on the inside and the outside, for God is at home in us.

Not only is His spirit available for His mighty power to direct and lead us in all areas of our life, but also, our bodies are designed for efficiency and long life. The Bible—

our wonderful Manual of Life—is the best recipe book and guidebook there is.

First Corinthians 6:19-20 tells us that we are to be good stewards of our own body. This can be described in a single word: ***discipline***. Don't let your body rule you; instead, you rule your body by good health habits.

Truly our bodies are magnificent machines, but they are so much better than manmade machines. God wants our bodies to be alive and vital, full of energy. We've been designed for a purpose, and God wants us to be healthy so that we're fully equipped for every good work He has in store for us.

We are to respect our bodies and care for them by supplying them with lots of pure water every day, eating fresh foods and vegetables that are as close as possible to being organic, and eliminating junk food and liquids that create toxicity. We are to get proper rest and exercise. We must be careful not to bombard our bodies with toxic chemicals and destructive habits that cause health problems and rob us of the life and energy the Lord wants us to have. We also must fill our minds with godly thoughts and thanksgiving to keep us healthy and to glorify the Lord.

Therefore, I encourage you to start this very today to learn all you can about preserving your greatest asset—your body.

The Bible and Divine Healing

Our God is a good God. He is not the author of suffering and sickness. He is a loving heavenly Father whose perfect will is for us to be healthy and whole. When we say that God is glorified in our sickness, we are inadvertently repeating a lie from the enemy. It is true that if we have a positive attitude and a word of praise to the Lord in our testimony while we're going through sickness and trauma of any kind, we will bring glory and honor to His name. Jesus ministered in town after town, preaching the Gospel, healing **all** manner of sickness and afflictions, opening the blind eyes, raising the dead, delivering from oppression, and casting out devils—**healing** every place He went. If He spent the last three years of His earthly life (His ministry years) healing **everyone** who came to Him, why would He, Almighty God, want to use sickness to bring glory to Himself? Not only that, Jesus gave *us* a commission to go out and do what He did. He even told us that *"He that believeth on me, the works that I do shall he do also; and greater works than these shall he do; because I go unto my Father" (**John 14:12**).* Healing is just as much a part of the atonement as the forgiveness of sins.

*"These signs shall follow them that believe; In my name shall they cast out devils; they shall speak with new tongues; They shall take up serpents; and if they drink any deadly thing, it shall not hurt them; they shall lay hands on the sick, and they shall recover" (**Mark 16:11-18**).*

In the first forty years of my Christian experience, the previous passage of Scripture was either ignored or someone would try to explain it away. Now I have learned better. The devil doesn't want us to know and believe the promises in the Bible about healing. He wants people to remain sick. Satan's *modus operandi* is death and destruction. Praise the Lord that the power of the Word in the name of Jesus heals and changes people.

Jesus is the same yesterday, today, and forever. It is difficult for me to understand how we can say we are Bible-believers and yet still not believe truly what Jesus did in His earthly ministry (signs, wonders, and healings), and do what He told us we should do. Yet I do understand because I was in that camp once and suffered because of my lack of knowledge and understanding. God is the same God today as the One who took care of His children in the wilderness. God does not tempt us with sin. God does not tempt with sickness. He can't. There is no darkness in Him. Sickness is darkness and suffering. It is limited death. Jesus took away our suffering and sickness on the cross. His atonement guarantees our victory. Jesus did it all for us at Calvary. We need to look boldly and honestly to the source of sickness. Sickness brings death. Jesus came to give life.

There are no "if it be your will" prayers in the Bible pertaining to healing. I am convinced that there is no faith from that course of prayer, but rather that it provides a "loophole" in case a person dies or we cannot explain it when our faith is lacking. We need to be bold in our faith and steadfast in the promises of the Word. It takes a determined trust. We are given the authority to command and use God's Word and the name of Jesus Christ.

Let us look at a very interesting passage of Scripture in Psalm 103:3: *"Who forgiveth all thine iniquities; who healeth all thy diseases."* For a Christian there is the sure knowledge that when we cry out to God to forgive us, we know that He hears us. Why is there such doubt and opposition to divine healing? Here we see that God puts them together. The same work on Calvary that atoned for our sins by the blood of Jesus made provision for our healing. When that truth gets into the spirit and heart, we will think differently. We will be able to say, "I *know* that I know that Jesus is my healer!"

I have learned about the power of supernatural healing. I've seen miracles happen to such an extent in my life through the power of the Word and in the name of Jesus that I am sold on what the Lord can and will do when we have absolute faith in Him. He is a God of miracles, and those miracles *ARE* available to us today.

*Is any among you afflicted? Let him pray. Is any merry? Let him sing psalms. Is any sick among you? Let him call for the elders of the church; and let them pray over him, anointing him with oil in the name of the Lord (**James 5:13-14**).*

Sickness starts in the mind. Notice the first *command* given in this verse: that we are to PRAY! What does the average Christian do when he begins to suffer more misery than he wants to handle, particularly sickness? He calls the doctor. Jesus says that we are to **pray**. He has given us authority, and we need to exercise it.

Notice the next phrase dropped right in the middle of that verse about how to handle sickness. I asked the Lord, "What about the statement about being merry?" Certainly sickness means enduring affliction and trouble, but the Lord reminded me of this verse: *"A merry heart doeth good like a medicine: but a broken spirit drieth the bones"* ***(Proverbs 17:22).*** What a truth to learn.

When most people are sick, they are not at their optimum energy level and thus they're usually prone to being on the grumpy side. Generally a sick person is not in the mood to give thanks. Often it seems as though we cannot give thanks simply because of how bad we are feeling. It seems a denial of the facts. The giving of praise is an attitude of the will. It requires believing what **God** can and will do. The Word says to *"call those things which be not as though they were"* ***(Romans 4:17).*** We are not denying the pain or discomfort and saying it is not real, nor are we trying to manipulate God into doing something. No; we are believing, by faith, that He will heal us as He promised. Operating in praise along with our faith is trusting with our spirit man. *"Rejoice evermore. Pray without ceasing. In every thing give thanks: for this is the will of God in Christ Jesus concerning you"* ***(1 Thessalonians 5:16-18).*** We are to give thanks for the promise. He tells us that He wants us to be in good health and to prosper. In Proverbs 4:22 God tells us the Word of God is health to our flesh. Lastly, we are to ask others to pray for us in our sickness. When you do ask them, however, get their assurance that they will not pray those doubting words of "if it be Thy will." Go to people who believe in the supernatural healing power of the Word of God.

We can learn some lessons on sickness from two Old Testament kings. One was King Asa, a good man who loved and served God. He rid the land of idols during his reign. He even had the courage to go against his mother's idols! But interestingly, he developed a severe disease in his feet. The Bible states that King Asa did not pray or seek God about the matter of his sickness, but instead he went to the physicians *first*. The next thing we read about King Asa is that he died. King Hezekiah had a sickness unto death. What did he do? He prayed with a contrite heart. The Lord heard him, healed him, and extended his life by fifteen years.

It is beneficial to learn these two scriptures until they are deep in your spirit. When they are, you will know, love, and claim these promises.

But he was wounded for our transgressions, he was bruised for our iniquities: the chastisement of our peace was upon him; and with his stripes we are healed **(Isaiah 53:5)**.

Who his own self bare our sins in his own body on the tree, that we, being dead to sins, should live unto righteousness: by whose stripes ye were healed **(1 Peter 2:24)**.

By the name of Jesus Christ we have been given authority over the enemy in all areas of our life, which includes attacks of sickness.

Please do not misunderstand me; it is not my intention to criticize medical science. I praise the Lord for medical science. There is a need and place for doctors and medical help. I am most thankful for them and for diagnostic equipment and insight. However, as Christians we are equipped to live on a higher plane, and that includes our wellness. *"And the very God of peace sanctify you wholly; and I pray God your whole spirit and soul and body be preserved blameless unto the coming of our Lord Jesus Christ"* ***(1 Thessalonians 5:23)*** and *"Beloved, I wish above all things that thou mayest prosper and be in health, even as thy soul prospereth"* ***(3 John 2).***

Why would Jesus want us afflicted with something when He has already died on the cross in order to deliver us? Think on this. It could set you free from all of your traditional and pre-conceived ideas and doctrines. It did me.

Granted, there will come a time, if it has not already happened, when a precious loved one, a dear friend, or an acquaintance will be taken suddenly from us, or a disease takes the life of a dear person even though there was much prayer and belief that they would recover. We do not understand why this happens and we may never know. We just have to leave it in the hands of God, because we know that everyone has a time to die. We should not blame or challenge the Lord. Be assured: if that person is a Christian, he/she is entering into a glorious eternity, and we can rejoice and be comforted in that knowledge. We are *"more than conquerors through Jesus Christ our Lord"* and *"...thanks be to God, which giveth us the victory through our Lord Jesus Christ"* ***(1 Corinthians 15:57).***

Please be kind to yourself and take care of your body and mind, for you are greatly loved. Also, be reminded that we are to be good stewards of our body and take care of it, for it is truly a magnificent machine. *"And the very God of peace sanctify you wholly; and I pray God your whole spirit and soul and body be preserved blameless unto the coming of our Lord Jesus Christ"* ***(1 Thessalonians 5:23).***

REVIEW

- Jesus not only provided redemption on the cross of Calvary, but He made provision for our healing and wellness.

The power of light will be revealed to us in the next chapter.

Chapter 12

CONSIDER THE CANDLE

To fully appreciate light, we need to understand the darkness. I recall when my oldest son worked as a guide at the Cave of the Winds in Manitou Springs, Colorado before going to college. One day he took us to experience the cave. I will never forget what it was like when the lights were turned off. Although it was only a matter of seconds, it seemed much longer. It was hard to keep from panicking in such total darkness, when you cannot see your own hand in front of you. It is easy for the imagination to run wild with thoughts of what could happen. What a relief when the lights were turned on once again.

I remember another time when I was visiting a dear friend who lives way back in the hill country of Texas. When the clouds cover the moon and stars at night it is pitch black. There are no city streetlights in that part of the country. We left the ranch house across the street from her home and did not have a flashlight. We knew there was heavy equipment to bump into and holes to cause us to fall or turn an ankle. Although she had walked that path often, we linked arms and inched our way down until we got to the street and could see a light in front of us that guided us home. It was a scary experience.

Darkness is the absence of light.
Oh, how we need the light.
Perhaps you experienced or read about the total blackout that occurred in New York City on July 13, 1977. The power went completely out and was not restored until late the following evening. There was panic and chaos in the city. People were trapped in buildings and elevators; looting and vandalism were rampant; over 1100 fires broke out (some of them multiple-alarm fires); thirty-five blocks of Broadway were destroyed; businesses were plundered and destroyed; jail cells could not hold all the arrests that were made; people could not get home to protect their properties; the subways and all transportation systems were utter chaos.

In 2003, forty million people in eight U. S. states suffered a blackout, and ten million people in Ontario, Canada were involved in the same blackout. The estimated damage in the U. S. alone was near the six billion dollar figure. Water contamination occurred because of the shutdown of water pumps with sewage spilling into waterways. Computers went down—and we all know that when computers go down, everything goes down. Power generation, manufacturing, transportation, and communication were all affected, to say nothing of home freezers filled with quickly spoiling food.

How important are light and power!
When I was a little girl, when the storms came and the power went out, it was time to pull out the candles, which were always kept in a specific place. Since we did not have a TV and the everyday use of computers was nonexistent, we didn't miss such things. I thought it was fun to play games by candlelight and enjoy the little adventure of feeling like a pioneer girl—**for a while.**

I remember one time when a major storm hit while we were living in Anchorage, Alaska, which knocked out the power for over a day. It was during the winter. We were a young married couple with a baby. We huddled in layers of clothes (no heat!), played games by candlelight, and ate sandwiches. It was fun—for about two or three hours. Then we began to feel the discomfort of having no electricity and heat.

Close your eyes for just a moment and try to imagine what it would be like to live in utter darkness. Our whole world would be without form and beauty. Aren't we grateful to be able to open our eyes and see light? These illustrations simply remind us that light and power are better than darkness and distress.

With one mighty word, God spoke and suddenly there was light. I believe He created light before creating anything else in order to demonstrate His mighty love for us. God loves us so much, and He demonstrates that love by *giving*. He gave the splendor of the universe for us to enjoy and visually see His love and power. Yes, God said let there be light, and there was light! Everything in God and of God is light. There is no darkness in Him—not even a particle of a particle.

- *God is light, and in him is no darkness at all* **(1 John 1:5)**.
- *Every good gift and every perfect gift is from above, and cometh down from the Father of lights, with whom is no variableness, neither shadow of turning* **(James 1:17)**.
- *The LORD is my light and my salvation; whom shall I fear? The LORD is the strength of my life; of whom shall I be afraid* **(Psalm 27:1)**.
- *For the LORD God is a sun and shield: the LORD will give grace and glory: no good thing will he withhold from them that walk uprightly* **(Psalm 84:11)**.

Satan is the one who possesses absolute darkness. Oh yes, he can momentarily appear as an angel of light, but it he always follows up this charade with darkness, death, and destruction. He knows that his future will be spent in the deep abyss of hell, and thus he wants to lure as many as he can into his chasm of darkness. Sin always brings darkness to the soul. That is the plan of the evil one. Sin is a serious business. It brings hurt to the heart, disease to the body, and confusion to the mind. Sin blocks out the light that God wants to shine into every human being.

I am reminded of the familiar story of the little frog that was put into a kettle of warm water. The little frog thought it was so nice and cozy. He lay back and floated with pleasure in his lukewarm environment. The heat was gradually turned up until it came to the place where the poor little frog was boiled to death. His cozy, lazy sense of "everything-is-alright" got the best of him. Are we like that? We do our own thing, always busy with this or that. We go to church on Sunday, get pumped up with a weekly sermon, and enjoy some good music. However, come Monday we go back to the comfortableness of our own schedule and we slip into the ungodly version of ourselves. We don't put God first in our life no matter how good we appear on the outside. We fail to consider the things that are so unholy to God. We get used to a "little bit of sin," –and we justify it by thinking, *after all, this is my life and my schedule.*

Darkness and sin are thrown in our faces every day. We cannot turn on the TV, read a newspaper, drive down the highway, or even walk into a grocery store without seeing someone or something that speaks of darkness rather than light. We can become so immune to it that we fail to speak out about it and reveal it for what it is. God says we are to hate the dark and love the light. *"Love not the world, neither the things that are in the world. If any man loves the world, the love of the Father is not in him. For all that is in the world, the lust of the flesh, and the lust of the eyes, and the pride of life, is not of the Father, but is of the world. And the*

world passeth away, and the lust thereof: but he that doeth the will of God abideth for ever" (1 **John 2:15-17**).
We cannot hide our secret sins. God knows what they are anyway! When we harbor sin and refuse to repent of it, we are going against our own soul. We are allowing darkness to come within us. The darkness will separate us from our loving, heavenly Father and keep us from walking in the beauty and joy of His Son, the Light. We need to repent and be cleansed often! God is for us, not against us. He knows how much we need His light and direction.

Jesus went into the very dark bowels of the earth and retrieved the keys of the kingdom in order that we may walk in light. Satan's darkness is now exposed. Jesus spoke this most marvelous truth and declaration: *"I am the light of the world: he that followeth me shall not walk in darkness, but shall have the light of life" (**John 8:12**).*

Light is a pure representation of God.

Before the days of fire ordinances and restrictions, I remember going to candlelight services, usually at Christmas time. Each person was given a candle. One person holding a burning candle started the light and it passed from person to person until everyone's candle was burning brightly. The candles spread a soft, beautiful yet brilliant glow throughout the darkened auditorium and gave a special presence to the gathering of worshippers. To a certain extent, the same thing is achieved nowadays with glow sticks or small flashlights, but somehow it is not quite the same as flickering candlelight.

For thousands of years in human history, campfires, candlelight, lamps, and lanterns were the only source of light after the sun went down. Torches lit the pathways. Fireplaces burnt brightly, creating a warm, welcoming gathering spot for the family.

We need to take a closer look at the word *candle* used in the Bible. The Hebrew (Young's entry #5216) and Greek translations of the word *candle* (Young's entry #3088) both define it as a ***lamp*** (particularly as the word is used in the King James Version of the Bible). So, wherever we see the word *candle* in the Bible, it is referring to a lamp. It is **very important for us to understand** this meaning and the difference.

The light given off by a lamp is very different from the light given off by a candle. The lamp will burn continually from a wick that floats within the oil. In Biblical times, they used bowls (lamps) filled with olive oil with wicks made from twisted plant fibers. Olive oil was readily available and inexpensive. There would be many lamps placed throughout the home, for one lamp only gave out the equivalent of a 40-watt bulb. Today in Israel you will see replicas of these bowls everywhere you go. In the finer antique stores of Israel, one might be able to purchase an original lamp (bowl); however, they are quite expensive and becoming more rare. Generally these small, flat bowl-shaped lamps are made from clay. In ancient times lamps were sometimes made of bronze or gold, but most of these were originally created for the wealthy. Some of the lamps were very ornate. All lamps were kept filled and the wicks trimmed so there would be continual light.

The candlestick mentioned in the Old Testament was actually a lampstand (Menorah) that held the oil and wick. The Menorah, a seven-branched candelabrum, is one of the oldest symbols of the Jewish faith. To the people of Israel the Menorah stands for their mission to be "the light of the world."

One of the functions of the priests of the Tabernacle was to keep the lamp filled with oil and the wick trimmed so that it would burn continuously. The lampstand of the Tabernacle was placed by the pattern of the Lord and carried great meaning, not only to the Jewish people, but also to those of us who have accepted Jesus, the Messiah, "the Light of the World." When we receive Jesus as our light, we are transferred from one kingdom to another. We are delivered from the power of darkness (Satan's territory) and translated into Jesus' kingdom of light. This is great good news—almost *too-good-to-be-true good news!* Why then, do we try to live so close to a dark kingdom and all it represents instead of placing both feet squarely into God's kingdom? Sadly, this is a practice of too many Christians. I believe it probably stems from a lack of truly understanding who they are and what they have in Christ.

There is a sweet song that is taught to most little children in Sunday school called "This Little Light of Mine." They hold up one precious little finger and sing:

> This little light of mine
> I'm going let it shine.
> This little light of mine
> I'm going to let it shine.
> Let it shine, let it shine, let it shine.
>
> Don't let Satan blow it out,
> I'm going to let it shine.
> Don't let Satan blow it out,
> I'm going to let it shine.
> Let it shine, let it shine, let it shine.

This little song is so simple, yet profound. All of God's children are to be a light in the darkness of this world. Each of us has a sphere of influence unlike anyone else's. We may be the only light and hope that another person has.

I am reminded of the lighthouses of old, before the time of electricity. Some lighthouses were isolated and difficult to get to, but they were always close to the harbor. The lighthouse keeper had the arduous and often lonely task of keeping the lighthouse in top condition. It was of utmost importance to keep the wicks trimmed and the lamps clean and filled with oil. The lighthouse was a guiding light to lead the ships safety into the harbor. The ship captain depended on that light on those dark or foggy nights. Even in the morning, fog can roll in and become dangerous. Without the light, the ship could be destroyed and life on board could be lost. No matter the weather or conditions, the keeper of the lighthouse had to do his job diligently.

Jesus is our lighthouse. We can draw an analogy from the lighthouse and its keeper to our responsibility as Christians. We are to be like the shining light of the lighthouse, taking the Gospel to our neighbor and around the world. The light of His presence is to shine through us and direct others to Him.

There is a most interesting verse of Scripture that states, *"For You (God) cause my lamp to be lighted and to shine; the Lord my God illumines my darkness"* **(Psalms 18:28 AMP)**. When we become His child, He puts within us His lamp that will search our soul to eliminate all the darkness within. This same lamp can be likened to the lamp that is full of oil, and the wick burning bright can be likened to the Holy Spirit who illuminates us and causes us to shine with power and give light to others. Like everything else, it is our choice to keep our lamp lit and shining brightly. *"Let your light so shine before men, that they may see your good works, and glorify your Father which is in heaven"* **(Matthew 5:16)**.

The Word of God is a *"lamp unto my feet and a light unto my path"* **(Psalm 119:105)**. We may be like a lighthouse, but if we do not put the Word into us daily, our lamp will become dim. The soot of sin must be cleaned away so that our light remains pure and bright. We are cleansed through the Word, which is our source and direction for all things. Our wick needs to continually be trimmed by the Lord so that the oil of the Holy Spirit can keep the flames burning.

We have also a more sure word of prophecy; whereunto ye do well that ye take heed, as unto a light that shineth in a dark place until the day dawn, and the day star arise in your hearts ***(2 Peter 1:19).***

I ask the following questions of myself. Would you like to join me?

- Am I living in darkness or light?
- Am I a candle or a lamp?
- What changes do I need to make in my life, starting today, to be a light in the darkness of this world?
- Yesterday or today, did I sit in front of TV for an hour and yet did not have time for God?
- Do I work diligently, or am I lazy and slothful?
- Am I a good steward of my possessions, and do I teach my children to appreciate what they have?
- Have I given time to ungodly things and neglected to seek holiness?
- How is my heart? Is it pure and clean or does it contain deceit and deception?
- Do I guard my mind against toxic thoughts? Am I putting good things into my mind?
- What comes out of my mouth? Are they words of praise and encouragement or words of judgment, anger, and harshness?
- Am I a thankful person or a complainer?
- Am I a giver or a taker?
- Am I perfecting a talent or ability, or do I say, "I'll start tomorrow."
- Do I live as though there is no tomorrow, or do I live as though this was my last day on earth?
- Am I looking forward to my heavenly home?

- Am I healthy and energetic or sick and worn out? If I am sick and worn out, what will I do to change this?
- Do I allow my body to rest, or am I always pushing it and under stress?
- Am I the center of my own universe?
- Do I see myself as God sees me, or do I carry guilt, inferiority, and failure?
- Am I fulfilling my dream or living in a nightmare?
- Do I truly love people or do I use them?
- Am I settling for a miserable today or a bright tomorrow?
- Am I creative, or do I feel inadequate?
- Is there anything in my possession that does not honor God?
- Am I living in debt? If so, am I willing to start today to make plans to be in financial freedom? (This is God's plan—He wants us out from under that burden.)
- Am I faithful to give a tenth of my income and more to the Lord's work?
- Am I content with what I have, or do I always need something else?
- Each one of us is a unique creation, not a carbon copy. Do I realize that this includes me?
- We are designed to love and not to lust.
- We are to be humble and not haughty.
- We are called to be servants, not self-seekers.
- We are to care and not to condemn.
- We were not created to be dropouts, diseased, or depressed, but to be vital, vibrant, and victorious.
- We are to be prosperous people and not paupers.
- We are created for purpose and productivity, not pointlessness.

We are capable to doing great things, because *"we can all things through Christ who strengthens us."*

I want to mention a very important principle to success. To some, it is an ugly four-letter work. It is called WORK! However, it is the root source of all success. Do you want a beautiful flower garden? I can guarantee you that it will require getting your hands dirty and pulling up weeds! A lovely manicured yard takes work. Is your home in order? If so, there has been some work involved. Do you want to be a good parent, spouse, and grandparent? It will mean forgetting about yourself and putting them first, even when you just don't *feel* like it. One has to WORK on relationships. Are you looking for success in the workplace? It will take determination, integrity, diligence, and WORK! Your dream will not come by sitting back and dreaming. You must work your dream. Do you say, "I want to know the Word of God and how to use it," or, "I want to pray effectively"? My friend, it takes an everyday, determined goal to study and learn what God says in His Word. (I would call this a working of the heart.) We don't learn how to win souls by just praying about it. We must *go and do it*, and that requires work. God gives gifts and talents to us, but we must develop them through the avenue of WORK. It is true in the natural realm and in the spiritual realm. Work is the opposite of slothfulness, laziness, sluggishness, and idleness:

- *Slothfulness casteth into a deep sleep; and an idle soul shall suffer hunger* **(Proverbs 19:15).**
- *He also that is slothful in his work is brother to him that is a great waste* **(Proverbs 18:9).**
- *Not slothful in business; fervent in spirit; serving the Lord* **(Romans 12:11).**

Does the Word say anything about work?

- *Whatsoever thy hand findeth to do, do it with thy might* **(Ecclesiastes 9:10).**

- *In all labour there is profit: but the talk of the lips tendeth only to penury [which means lack], need, poverty, want* **(Proverbs 14:23).**
- *Whereunto I also labour, striving according to his working, which worketh in me mightily* **(Colossians 1:29).** From the **Amplified Version:** *For this I labor [unto weariness], striving with all the superhuman energy which He so mightily enkindles and works within me.*
- *Let him that stole steal no more: but rather let him labour, working with his hands the thing which is good, that he may have to give to him that needeth* **(Ephesians 4:28).**
- *And that ye study to be quiet, and to do your own business, and to work with your own hands, as we commanded you* **(1 Thessalonians 4:11).**

On the road to success we need to be aware of dangers. These are not the usual dangers we might consider. They are very subtle and we might even miss them, but they are dangers, nonetheless.

Danger #1 – Be on guard after you've had a spiritual mountaintop experience. Yes, put that experience into your memory bank and write it down, but do not let it be your guide. The enemy is always waiting at the foot of the mountain. Keep all experiences grounded by the Word of God.

Danger #2 – Be careful how you receive compliments and praise. All of us should strive to be encouragers, and everyone needs encouragement at one time or another in their life. However, compliments and praise can be a heady experience and cause us to get sidetracked.

Danger #3 – Making emotional decisions. They can lead to trouble down the road.

Danger #4 – Credit card debt. It will surely come back to haunt you.

Danger #5 – Be careful of a bonus or financial blessing. Make sure it is spent wisely.
Danger #6 – Pride. It comes before destruction. It is something God hates.
Danger #7 – Seeking to be served rather than to serve.
Danger #8 – Being too busy for God to develop a personal relationship with Him.
Danger #9 – Going through daily life without prayer and Bible study. Too many mistakes will be made.
Danger #10 – Having a passive attitude when you need to be proactive.
Danger #11 – Measuring yourself against someone else and their accomplishments.
Danger #12 – Busy with much service and church activity but having no real surrender in your heart to the Lordship of Jesus.
Danger #13 – Judging others and making false assumptions about them. You may not know the whole story.
Danger #14 – To get to a place in your life where you stop learning.
Danger #15 – Being too hasty to believe everything you hear.
Danger #16 – Neglecting your body, soul, and mind.
Danger #17 – Quitting too soon.

I am sure you can add to this list. On every journey of life, there will be dangers and roadblocks along the way. However, a watchful eye will guard against many pitfalls.

REVIEW

- Write down goals for those things you desire to achieve in this journey of life.
- Record scriptures that spoke to you in the reading of this chapter.

Chapter 13

SHIELD OR ROPE – WHICH WILL YOU CHOOSE?

*P*icture a man who is holding on to a rope that is dangling over a limb above a swollen, rushing river. His survival instincts are in full gear and he is struggling to maintain a grip. He is hanging on for dear life, and there is no protection from the elements around him. He constantly sways back and forth and is beaten by tree limbs and bugs flying through the air. He is crying out for help but it seems as though no one hears him. He is desperate for someone to come to his rescue.

Imagine someone whose life is in total disarray. Despair has taken hold of them, and the ever-descending darkness of depression seems to block out any ray of hope. Suicide seems like a viable alternative in the mind of this oppressed and confused person. Suicide is never the answer, but desperation within the human soul can be so overwhelming as to cause the one struggling with it to lose the natural, instinctive desire to live. Faith and hope have long since fled their soul and spirit.

Many are living a life of enduring, hanging on with all their might to get through their daily existence, wondering if things will ever get better. They are hanging on to their "rope." They do not have joy in their life, and their existence is empty and seemingly futile. Their life can seem very busy to someone on the outside looking in, but at the end of the day, there is the reality of emptiness.

Along comes a witness. He speaks of the great gulf between lost man and Almighty God. The witness gives hope that there is a bridge between the two, and His name is Jesus. Salvation is fully supported by the cross of Calvary. Repentance and acceptance is the answer. The words that the witness shares are new and strange, but something rises within the listener's soul—the conviction of sin. The message is believed and he reaches out to accept Jesus. What happens when repentance and belief meet? A life is transformed. Why? Because God gives every man, woman, boy, and girl the faith to become born again. What has formerly been unknown is now the glorious acceptance of a new way and the start of an exciting journey. How does someone receive this new life in Christ? By grace through faith in God.

We observe Christians who are so bound down by circumstances and defeat that they, too, seem to barely be hanging on by an invisible rope. They may be going through the motions at church and even participating in many of the functions of church involvement, but at home they feel rejected and defeated. How can this be? The child of God is to live a life of expectancy with joy and hope and FAITH. If you sense that these paragraphs are describing your inner struggles, please know that the answer to this question may hold the key to being set free: In which house are you living, the house of self or the house of faith?

Volumes have been written about faith. However, the intent of this book is to give you thought-provoking nuggets that will challenge you to search and make real this adventure of living successfully by faith. It is my heart's desire that you will be successful and grow in faith. I want you to have victory over the obstacles you are facing.

Every Christian has been given a measure of faith (Romans 12:3). When one has been changed by the power of the Gospel, faith is put into him because of God's amazing grace. It is part of the package deal. God clearly demands faith. He declares that **without faith it is impossible to please Him.** Remember what we learned about God: He cannot lie. His Word never, ever changes. He is true and faithful. His immutable laws are always in place. He has given us a new "bank account of heaven" with promissory notes ready to be claimed by His children. Therefore, if He demands that we live by faith, then He has already provided a way for us to receive this faith.

Since we are told emphatically that without faith it is impossible to please God (Hebrew 11:1), and that we must believe that God **is** and that He rewards those who seek Him, then we must come to a full understanding of the meaning of faith in order to reach for it and believe it can be ours.

The Bible is its own best commentary. Remember this principle as you study the Word, for it will give you a witness in Scripture. *"Now faith is the substance of things hoped for, the evidence of things not seen" **(Hebrews 11:1).*** The key word in this verse is *substance*. The meaning of the word *substance* in the Greek language is: "that which has foundation; is firm; that which has actual existence; real being – a substance; confidence, assurance, firm trust." *Webster's Dictionary* gives this meaning: "Something real, not imaginary; something solid, not empty; the essential part; the main or material part." The second part of the verse speaks of the evidence of things not seen. Evidence is: *a proof; that by which a thing is tested or proved.* Andrew Wommack states it so well when he says**, "Faith is our positive response to what God has already done. Grace has to be mixed with faith."**

Clearly, the Lord wants to help us and bless us. We are to respond in obedience to Him. We must trust and believe in what He says and then take positive action. This truth is presented so clearly in James 1:5-6, where we are promised wisdom, liberally, but we must ask in faith and not waver. If we waver, we're like the waves of the sea driven by wind and tossed about. Have you ever watched the strong winds of a storm churn everything in the water, sometimes causing objects to fly high in the air and slam onto the shore? This is what James is telling us—that without faith our prayers will go unanswered, and we will have turbulence within because of our unbelief.

In the sixth chapter of Ephesians we learn that we have a spiritual suit of armor that was given to us when we were saved. The Bible refers to it as the whole armor of God. It is comprised of the belt of truth; the breastplate of righteousness; sandals of peace; the helmet of salvation; and two moveable pieces of protection—one is the Sword of the Spirit, which is the Word of God, and the other is the shield of faith. In all of this we are to put on the "Lord Jesus Christ" as we would put on a cloak or our hand in a glove. This is our garment of protection against the enemy.

We will now consider our shield of faith. The Greek word for **shield** is *Thureos*: a large oblong, four-cornered shield. This comes from the Greek word *thura*, or door. The shield was made from a frame of wood covered with several layers of leather or rawhide nailed securely in place. The shield was 2 ½ to 3 feet wide and 4 ½ to 5 feet high. When the soldiers went into battle they would soak their shields in water. The weapons of the enemy were darts or arrows that had been dipped in pitch or tar and set on fire. Thus, the shield became a personal fortress to the soldier.

Romans soldiers were the leaders in war strategy during that era of history. The soldiers would line up shield-to-shield with just a small slit in between the shields for the sword to go through. Then, as a mighty walled fortress, the soldiers would move forward as one in their defense against the enemy. The shields were impenetrable to the fiery darts and arrows. What a marvelous illustration of the defense that is ours.

We know that Satan is always throwing his fiery darts in our direction, trying to hinder or destroy us, but when our shield of faith is in place, those dangerous darts just drop off.

This shield is more than just an instrument of defense for the Christian; it is Jesus Himself (Psalms 33:20, Proverbs 30:5). What a comfort to know that He is our shield and He is doing battle for us. If God is for us, who can be against us? If we are feeling overwhelmed by the enemy's attacks, it would be a good idea to stop and check our armor to see if there are any holes in it. Make sure the shield of faith is in place. If the shield is down, there is no protection. This is true for all of the weapons of our spiritual warfare. As long as our suit of armor stays in the closet it is of no benefit to us. We have to take the armor out of storage and actually put it on to be fully prepared against the enemy.

Annette Capps, a student of Quantum Physics and a Bible teacher, gives this very interesting concept of faith on her booklet *Quantum Faith:* "By comparing quantum physics with spiritual laws, I want to present you a different way of thinking, and by doing so open a whole new avenue and understanding of the faith that moves mountains.

Faith is an unseen energy force. It is not matter, but it creates matter and actually becomes matter. The faith that you use to call forth the manifestation of healing or finances changes form when the manifestation takes place. That is because faith-energized words convert energy to matter. Words are the catalyst that turns the substance of faith into physical manifestation. Faith is the raw material from which all matter is made. Hebrews 11:1 says, *"Faith is the substance..."* It is the invisible substance from which your physical world was and is created.

God used faith-substance and word-energy to create the universe. He spoke and the vibration (sound) of His words released the substance that became the stars and planets.

Words are the carrier of substance. They carry the substance to wherever it is directed. If you direct your faith toward your bank account with the intention of filling it to overflowing, then your word-energy vibrations will cause your bank account to become a magnet for the substance of money. Money (substance) will begin to come to you from a variety of different sources.

If you direct your faith to the healing of your body, then your words will carry healing energy to the cellular level of your body. On the vibrations of your words, faith-substance is carried to your body where it then becomes healing-substance.

Just as God created the universe by faith-substance and word-energy, you create your own universe by your faith and your words. If you don't like what you have created, you can change it!

While contemplating this chapter I was reflecting on some of the great saints of the faith. I thought to myself, Gal, you certainly are not in that line-up!" Then truth hit me again. I *do* have the same faith. I have as much right to believe and accept what God has given me as the greatest Christians the world has ever known. It is a matter of exercising that faith. Isn't that an incredible revelation!

I have experienced enough about faith to know that I want to grow and claim all the promises and protection God has given me. It is my heritage and my right as His daughter. One day I was reminded of Hebrews 11:1 as I was driving my car and considering this chapter. I started quoting it aloud several times, and each time I would put emphasis on a different word in the verse. (Doing this helps to seal the truth of this scripture verse in your spirit.):

- **WITHOUT** faith it is impossible to please God.
- Without **FAITH** it is impossible to please God.
- Without faith it is **IMPOSSIBLE** to please God.
- Without faith it is impossible **TO PLEASE GOD**.

Within a short time faith began to rise up in me. I thought of the many times in the past when I trusted God's Word and how the Lord helped me as a result of my faith. Over and over again, I have seen His promises work on a daily basis. I have experienced my own healings; I've seen other people healed and come out of wheel chairs; I've had dramatic answers to prayers; protection has been provided; storms have stopped; and supernatural provisions have been made. When I have put my trust in God's promises and believed they would come to pass, I have been given guidance and specific direction when faced with difficult decisions, and I have seen impossible projects materialize and more! As I drove along that day quoting Hebrews 11:1 aloud, I became excited all over again about the awesome God I serve!

I remembered another moment when a little song came to me as I was driving down I-35 to Dallas. That particular time in my life was a challenging one, and I was talking to the Lord about my problems as I was driving along. Then a little song of faith came to me. I had not heard the song in years, yet the Lord knew I needed it at that very moment. My faith was lifted as I sang this chorus.

> Got any rivers you think are uncrossable?
> Got any mountains you can't tunnel through?
> God specializes in things thought impossible
> He can do what others cannot do!

> - Oscar Eliason

We sometimes feel like our problem or circumstance is impossible. However, we serve the God of the impossible! The impossible can become positive, peaceful proof when we put our trust in the Lord's promises and view our circumstances through the eyes of faith. Remember this promise: *"We call those things that be not, as though they were" (Romans 4:17).*

All too often we hear negative "why?" questions, such as. "Why didn't you help me, God?" "Why did this happen to me?" "Why hasn't God answered my prayer?" "If God is so good why does He allow this to happen?" "Why doesn't God love me?" Why, Why, Why? The answer to the question is in the fact that Jesus did it all on Calvary. All provisions were made for everything we need in this life because of His atonement. What grace! We see in the very beginning that God said the heavens were His, but He gave the earth to man. God put all the laws and principles in place for us, but we have made a colossal mess of things. Could it be that we are not living in obedience to what has been promised to us? God will not do for us what He expects us to do. Don't forget—He did not turn us into puppets or robots when we got saved. He equipped us and gave us the promises to act upon. He is ready, willing, and abundantly able to act on our behalf, but we need to exercise active, living faith in Him first. We can say beautiful prayers to the ears of others as well as ourselves that sound so spiritual, when in reality they are of little or no value unless the ingredient of faith and love is the motivation behind those prayers. Faithless praying gets no higher than the ceiling. Just as your house is wired for electricity, but you can only receive its benefits when you turn on the switch, so it is with praying. The power is there but faith is the switch. Faith calls for an action in the spirit.

The eleventh chapter of Hebrews is called 'the faith chapter'. It is most interesting to read those listed in the Great Hall of Faith. There is one person who really blesses me. In this list of heroes and heroines of the faith, we see Rahab. It is rather attention grabbing to note that she is always referred to in Scripture as Rahab the Harlot. She was a Canaanite and could have been a temple prostitute. How would you like to be identified and addressed by your most notorious sin? It would be like going to someone and saying, "I would like you to meet Marvin, the Murderer." Or ... how about this for an introduction: "I would like you to know Glenna the Gossiper?" We get the idea. Rahab the Harlot's story reassures us that if Rahab can be blessed, anyone can!

Rahab heard about the great exploits of the God of Israel and she believed in Him. She was aware of the fear her people had of the Israelites. Yes, she believed in this God, and as a result, faith would soon rise up in her heart to put that belief in action. When the men who were spies for Israel came to her home, she hid them from the king's soldiers. Rahab's home was strategically placed on the great wall of the city. The spies of Israel and Rahab made a covenant. If she would not betray the men's whereabouts but instead would help them hide, they promised to protect her from destruction when the battle came against her city. Rahab was not just concerned about herself but for all of her family, so she asked for their safety as well. This speaks volumes about Rahab's heart and courage. She was willing to risk her life for others. Eventually she let the men down from a scarlet rope and told them to hide for three days. The scarlet rope was left in place to identify her house when later the Israelites would take over the city.

You can imagine what it was like in Rahab's house when the walls started tumbling down. The little children were probably crying, huddled around terror-stricken parents. The house was vibrating and shaking with dishes and objects flying through the room. It was a most frightening moment. I can see Rahab hugging them and praying, assuring her family that everything would be okay. She believed her God would take care of them. When the mighty walls of Jericho came tumbling down, her house stood. What a miracle! The promise the spies had made to her concerning her family's safety and protection was kept. Rahab and all of her relatives in the home were spared. They left the ruins of Jericho and went to live with the Israelites because of the faith of one woman.

So often people, even among Christians, are judged by how they look, their impressive resume, or their social status. The average churchgoer would not have elected Rahab the Harlot to such an honorable position. In fact, most would not even choose to be associated with her. God thought so much of her that her deeds were recorded in the Eternal Book, and she is found in the lineage of our Savior, Jesus Christ.

God uses the foolish things of this world to confound the wise. All He wants is willing vessels. As we read about the men and women of faith mentioned in Hebrews 11, we see that many had serious character deficiencies at one time in their lives: murder, lying, deception, and cowardice to name a few. But the point is that God that looks on the heart and knows whether or not faith is real. Even before Calvary, His mercy was always there to love and forgive. He used imperfect people then and continues to do so today. There is no such thing as a perfect person serving the Lord. Only Jesus is perfect. Praise the Lord for Calvary and the promise that *"If we confess our sins, He is faithful and just to forgive us of our sins and cleanse us from all unrighteousness"* **(1 John 1:9)**. What a loving and merciful Lord we serve! We are all under sin, and it is by the promise of faith in Jesus Christ that we can believe (Galatians 3:22). Grace, grace, marvelous grace has been given to ALL people. Praise the Lord for the power of the Holy Spirit and the changes He produces within us.

I lived in the same house and had the same bedroom from the time I was a baby until I graduated from high school (a rarity these days!). Someone gave me a small plaque that hung on the walls for years. It reminds me of the futility of worry, which is the opposite of faith.

> Said the robin to the sparrow
> I would really like to know;
> Why these anxious humans being
> Rush about and worry so.
> Said the sparrow to the robin,
> Surely it must be
> That they have no heavenly Father
> Such as cares for you and me!

Doesn't that sound like us at times? We find ourselves struggling and striving as though everything depends on us, when in spiritual reality what we need is faith that totally depends on God. We think it depends on *our* good plan or program to get the job done. Unbelief says that Jesus can't really help us; surely He needs our abilities! Unbelief among the people in His own country kept Jesus from doing miracles there. What a tragedy. We need to realize that everything has already been done for us—EVERYTHING. We need to rest in Him and find joy in this fact. The wonderful hymn tells us "Jesus paid it all; all to Him we owe."

If we can figure out a situation using our own five senses and intellect, we are probably not exercising much faith unless we prayed beforehand and know that the Lord is directing us in that situation. Again, we do not grow our faith by our efforts, hard work, and religious activity, or by our moral and upright standing. Faith comes by hearing and doing the Word of God. It comes by supernatural intervention.

Do you know that God does not answer our prayer based on our wants or our begging and pleading? The Lord cares about the anguish of our heart, but the key to receiving answers to prayer is by choosing the avenue of faith. What a blessing to have access to the supernatural through the Holy

NEVER GIVE UP

Spirit. Faith is an action word. We must know His Word, act upon it in faith, and receive the promise by total trust in what He has said. Our faith must come BEFORE the reality of the answer appears. *"But be ye doers of the word, and not hearers only, deceiving your own selves" (James 1:22).* There is a great key in the words 'deceiving ourselves'. We are to test what we think and determine if we are deceived or not. *"But without faith it is impossible to please him: for he that cometh to God must believe that he is, and that he is a rewarder of them that diligently seek him"* **(Hebrews 11:6).**

Great statements of faith from God's children:

Abraham: *"My God will provide a lamb" (Genesis 22:8).*
Caleb: *"Lord, give me this mountain" (Joshua 14:12).*
David: *"The Lord will deliver me from the hand of the Philistine"* **(1 Samuel 17:37).**
Job: *"I know my redeemer lives" (Job 19:25).*
Paul: *"Be of good cheer for I believe God that it shall be even as it was told me" (Acts 27:25).*
The leper: *"Lord, you can make me clean" (Matthew 8:2).*
The blind man: When Jesus asked him if he could be healed, he replied "Yes, Lord" *(Matthew 9:28).*
The woman with the issue of blood: *"If I can touch his clothes, I will be healed" (Mark 5:27).*
The centurion: *"Speak the word only, and my servant shall be healed" (Matthew 8:8).*
Stephen: He was full of so much faith and power that *"the people were not able to resist the wisdom and spirit by which he spoke" (Act. 6:8).*
Jesus: He had absolute faith in His Heavenly Father, and whatever God the Father told Him to do, He did.

Remember, whatever is *not* of faith is sin, but what *is* of faith is righteousness: *It is better to trust in the LORD than* to put confidence in man *(Psalm 118:8). Commit thy way unto the LORD; trust also in him; and he shall bring it to pass (Psalm 37:5).*

Enemies of faith to be on guard against:
Doubt – The word doubt in the Greek language is simply defined as "to waiver." Webster's definition is "to be hesitant, uncertain." The Bible says that he that doubts is damned or judged, and that *"Whatsoever is not of faith is sin" (Romans 14:23).* This is because doubt ties the hand of God. First Timothy 2:8 teaches us what God wants us to do: *"I will therefore that men pray every where, lifting up holy hands, without wrath and doubting."*

Unbelief – Unbelief has a stronger meaning: "unfaithfulness, faithless; want of faith, weakness of faith." It's relevant to point out once again that even Jesus could not do miracles in His own country because of the unbelief of the people there.

Romans 3:3 declares, *"For what if some did not believe? Shall their **unbelief** make the faith of God without effect?"* God describes an unbelieving heart as *evil,* and He gives strong warning about it.

"Take heed, brethren, lest there be in any of you an evil heart of unbelief, in departing from the living God" (Hebrews 3:12). We must guard our heart diligently against this evilness. The mind and conscience can become defiled with unbelief (see Titus 1:15). Clearly, doubt and unbelief are serious matters with God.

Fear – The word 'fear' is defined as "to be afraid: to be struck with fear, to be seized with alarm; to flee."

Fear can be a strong spirit that is constantly working against us. Fear can paralyze us and cause us to believe a lie. It can give false symptoms and make us weary, tired, and troubled. Fear can cause us to believe a bad report. Fear is a trap of the enemy. We are not to fear, because *"God hath not given us the spirit of fear; but of power, and of love, and of a sound mind"* **(2 Timothy 1:7).**

Forasmuch then as the children are partakers of flesh and blood, he also himself likewise took part of the same; that through death he might destroy him that had the power of death, that is, the devil **(Hebrews 2:14).**

More enemies of faith:
- Trusting in our own abilities works, plans, and programs **(Philippians 3:9; Zechariah 4:6)**
- Rising up in proud independence instead of depending on the Lord **(Hebrews 10:38)**
- Sin **(Romans 14:23)**
- Trusting in emotions rather than the Word. Where there is anger, timidity, complaining, faultfinding, evil speaking, over-extended grief, an unforgiving spirit, and unbelief, faith is not present. **(John 6:63)**

It is the spirit that quickeneth; the flesh profiteth nothing: the words that I speak unto you, they are spirit, and they are life **(John 6:63).**

When you find yourself losing faith, remember that Satan will use all of these tactics against you in such a way that will make you think it is all your fault and is a result of your wrong thinking. He *continually* fights against faith that honors God, because he knows that is where he is defeated.

Faith that works.
Those of great faith are in the Word of God on a daily basis. We must know the Word. Confessing a matter over and over does not produce faith; rather, it is the confession of faith *based* on the Word that does so.

Therefore, if we do not know the Word, how can we confess it?

- Faith comes by hearing the Word. **(Romans 10:17)**
- Faith works by love. **(Galatians 5:6)**
- Faith is essential in our prayer life, and it gives us wisdom. **(James 1:5-6)**
- We are to live by faith. **(2 Corinthians 5:7; Romans 1:17)**

It is our faith that releases God to extend His grace to us.
- All things are possible by faith. **(Mark 11:23-24)**
- Faith must be activated by our spoken words of authority. **(Mark 11:23)**
- We are established by faith. **(Colossians 2:6-7)**
- We are to put on faith. **(1 Thessalonians 5:8)**
- We are to be strong in faith. **(Romans 4:19-20)**
- We have power in faith. **(Mark 11:23)**
- We overcome the enemy by our faith. **(1 John 4:4; Revelation 12:1)**
- We must know that Jesus is the Author and Finisher of our faith. **(Hebrews 23:2)**

There is no testimony without a test.
It has been said that there is no testimony without a testing. Life has challenges and obstacles as well as suffering. You may be in a sea of tranquility at this moment, but it is a sure thing that the winds of adversity will blow. Without an anchor of faith, you will be tossed back and forth.

Those who've been used greatly of God also went through the most difficult trials. We certainly see this in the life of the saints listed in the Bible in Hebrews 11. Those of great faith had dark, silent moments of testing, times of seeming delays to answered prayer or perhaps great physical struggles. It is through the challenges of life and the times of testing that we are purified and refined the precious gold.

We know that a diamond in the rough is not beautiful when it's first extracted from the earth. To the inexperienced eye it could easily be mistaken for just a dirty rock. It must go through a cleaning process, polishing, and precise cutting before it is transformed into a priceless gem. It takes the time and skill of a master artist to bring about such a transformation. The refining process comes before gold or precious metal is brought to its final form. Lovely pottery has to be molded and shaped, then fired in a kiln at an extremely high temperature. Without the firing process there would be nothing more than crumbling clay.

How would we feel if we were in Abraham's shoes as he walked up the mountain with his son in preparation for sacrificing him, wood in hand? In the three days it would take to make the journey, would our mind be going over the awful moment ahead of us when the knife would be thrust into our beloved son? Would we watch our son as he slept, thinking of precious times we'd spent with him? Would we feel the agony of knowing this would be the last time we would see him? Most of us would absolutely lose it if our precious son looked us in the eye and said "Daddy, where is the lamb for the sacrifice?" But Abraham believed God! There must have been a deep sense of peace within him as he believed His God would provide a lamb or raise his son from the dead. His faith allowed him to tell his servants that he and his son would be back. Jehovah-Jireh was there all the time, before the plan, during the plan, and after the plan.

Daniel and the three young Hebrew men were not given any "end-of-story" information when they were led to that horrible fire. They could feel the intense heat and see the rising flames. They could imagine what their fate would be like. There could have been a moment of fear before the calm assurance of faith set in. *But* ... they believed in their

God with an undeniable faith. When they were in the midst of the roaring fire, they saw the figure of a fourth Man who hadn't gone into the furnace with them. Who was there with them? The Lord himself was there in the fire, before the fire, and after the fire.

We don't know all the circumstances of the woman with the issue of blood, but we do know that she was determined to get to Jesus. Her faith told her she would be healed if she could just touch the hem of His garment. She was very sick and it doesn't say there was anyone to help her. Perhaps she had to get down on her hands and knees and crawl through the crowd toward Jesus. Maybe her hands and knees were bloodied. Possibly she was laughed at and faced contempt as she pulled herself along. She could have faced the fear of being trampled to death. As she labored through the crowd, her faith kept pressuring her on to the Healer. She knew if she touched the hem of Jesus' garment she would be healed. Jesus was there. The woman's faith touched the heart of the Savior as she touched the hem of His garment. She was made whole. Praise the Lord.

We can study the lives of the heroes of the faith and see hardships that were endured before the victory was won (see Hebrews 11:33-40).

The process of adversity shapes our character. Accomplishments are usually preceded by work and failures. Often, it is the failures that give us endurance and teach us important lessons on the pathway to success. We are given assignments without having any knowledge of what the end result will be. We must start, and by all means—we must finish.

We can know that God is always with us during the trials of our faith. He will never leave us or forsake us. He honors His covenant to us. Jesus is the same yesterday, today, and forever. He is the foundation rock that holds our house secure in the midst of the storms of life. We can literally cast every care, circumstance, and difficulty on Him because He is the Creator of the universe and knows the end from the beginning. He loves us and wants to see us blessed. We may feel the darkness, but He is all light. Satan might try to hinder us, but *"greater is He that is in us!"* We can put all of our trust in Almighty God. *"And we know that all things work together for good to them that love God, to them who are the called according to his purpose"* **(Romans 8:28).** Note the condition: To **love God** and be **called** according to His purpose.

It is never fun when your faith is being tested, but the trial will work patience, experience, and hope. Praising the Lord with thankfulness lifts the heart during the hard times. The blessings and miracles that follow the trials are far above all we could ask or think. Not only will we be blessed, but others will be as well. *"That the trial of your faith, being much more precious than of gold that perisheth, though it be tried with fire, might be found unto praise and honour and glory at the appearing of Jesus Christ"* **(1 Peter 1:7).**

Knowing this, that the trying of your faith worketh patience. But let patience have her perfect work, that ye may be perfect and entire, wanting nothing. If any of you lack wisdom, let him ask of God, that giveth to all men liberally, and upbraideth not; and it shall be given him **(James 1:3-5 AMP).**

There is a battle that we are told to fight. It is called the good fight of faith. *"**Fight** (Greek meaning: contend, struggle with difficulties and dangers, endeavour with strenuous zeal, strive, to obtain something) the good fight (Greek meaning: the place of the contest or battle) of faith"* **(1 Timothy 6:12).** This is a fight that we know we will win because it is not ours; it is the Lord's. *"If we continue in the faith grounded and settled, and be not moved away from the hope of the gospel..."* **(Colossians 1:23).** The condition is **IF**. We must exercise our faith. We already know the end of the Book, and we win.

Mighty Prayers

- *Wherefore also we pray always for you, That our God would count you worthy of this calling, And fulfill all the good pleasure of his goodness, And the work of faith with power* **(2 Thessalonians 1:11 AMP)**
- *But ye, beloved, building up yourselves on your most holy faith, praying in the Holy Ghost* **(Jude 1:20)**.
- *[And I pray] that the participation in and sharing of your faith May produce and promote full recognition and appreciation and understanding and precise knowledge of every good [thing] that is ours in [Our identification with] Christ Jesus [and unto His glory]* **(Philemon 6 AMP)**.

Mighty Answers

- *Hitherto have ye asked nothing in my name: ask, and ye shall receive, that your joy may be full* **(John 16:24)**.
- *In whom we have boldness and access with confidence by the faith of him* **(Ephesians 3:12)**.

Let's take a moment to consider what God is saying to us in this verse: *"I call heaven and earth to record this day against you, that I have set before you life and death, blessing and cursing: therefore choose life, that both thou and thy seed may live"* **(Deuteronomy 30:19)**.

As Andrew Wommack puts it so succinctly, in this verse "God is giving us a no-brainer quiz."

a) Choose life
b) Choose death

And then He gives the answer:

a) Choose life

It is our choice to exercise doubt or faith, to lose or win. Let's choose to live by faith!

We are coming close to the end of this book. Dear reader, you are the reason for all that it contains. Thank you for taking the journey with me. It is my sincere desire that within these pages you have found some keys that will unlock the doors of your heart and give you a desire to have a new, transformed life of abundance, the kind that money cannot buy.

I want to express, again, the love of God and how much He cares for you. Our finite understanding of love pales in comparison to the genuine love the Lord has for us. He loves us with an everlasting love (Jeremiah 31:3), and He draws us to Himself. God delights in us (Isaiah 62:4). What an awesome truth! God desires to do things for us. When we fully grasp the depth of this love, our life is changed. Truly this knowledge must come from a revelation of the Spirit to the individual heart.

Our Lord is magnificent and holy, and yet He is Abba Father, our daddy. The journey of life under His direction is marvelous. We have this promise: *"they that seek the* L<small>ORD</small> *shall not want any good thing"* **(Psalms 34:10)**. We do not have to lack *anything*. Everyone desires to have peace, love, and joy in their life, but these do not come from money, fame, accolades, talent, and abilities. No; these come from living a surrendered life to the Lord Jesus. The key to abundance is found in the seeking of Him. He will give us those things that are a blessing in abundance. Everyone has a creative gift.

We are in the world but not of this world. We are to be a happy, joyful people influencing those around us for good. The normal Christian life is one of the supernatural. If we are grumpy, self-centered, and sensitive, then we are giving the wrong reflection of God. We are to live in His power as a shining light to make a difference to all those with whom we come in contact. You might be thinking *this just sounds too hard*. You'll discover, however, that it's not hard at all with the Lord's empowering. When we allow God to be the God of our life, He provides infuses His energy and power into our efforts and fills our *lamps* to overflowing. The Christian life is the only way to be truly successful. The flesh will fade and die away; only the things of the Spirit are everlasting.

This is such a mighty promise to each of us: *And to know the love of Christ, which passeth knowledge, that ye might be filled with all the fulness of God. Now unto him that is able to do exceeding abundantly above all that we ask or think, according to the power that worketh in us, unto him be glory in the church by Christ Jesus throughout all ages, world without end. Amen **(Ephesians 3:19-21)**.*

May the title of this book, *Never Give Up,* resonate in your heart and mind as you persevere in living the spirit-filled Christian life. Push forward until you accomplish the purpose for which God created you.

In conclusion, if you **Never Give Up** in applying the principles found in the Manual of Life, God's Holy Word, you will find the real secret of success. It is my heart's desire for this to be true of everyone who reads this book. May the Lord richly bless you.

Bibliography

American Academy of Childhood and Adolescent Psychiatry, *Children and TV Watching*, http://www.aacap.org, #54 March 2001

http://www.brainconnection.com/

Capps, Annette. *Quantum Faith*. Capps Publishing, 2005

Capps, Charles. *The Tongue, A Creative Force*. Capps Publishing.

http://www.cymaticsource.com/

http://en.wikipedia.org/wiki/Hans_Jenny_(pedologist)

Eastman, Dick. *World Literature Crusade*.

www.cacmboston.org/pdf/resources/HowToSpendAnHourInPrayer

Espinosa, Eddie Mercy/Vineyard Publishing, http://www.worship.co.za/series/cmh-0101.asp

Hill, Stephen L., *Daily Awakenings*. Regal Books, 1999

Hormann, Dr. Aiko, *Overcomers' Guidebook*. Aiko Hormann Ministries International.

Hormann, Dr. Aiko, *Understanding Triggering Mechanisms,* Aiko Hormann Ministries International, 1975.

Leaf, Dr. Caroline, "Who Switched Off Your My Brain," Switch On Your Brain Organisation, PTY (Ltd), 2007

Pert, Dr. Candace, *Molecules of Emotion,* UK: Simon and Schuster, 1997. http://www.candacepert.com/

Ryabinow, Alyosha. "Hebrew, the Language from Heaven!" *Mishpochah,* March 2007.

Stowell, Dr. Jerome. http://www.gilead.net/bibletopics/bodypower.html

Wommack, Andrew Ministries International. *Bible Commentary.* http://www.awmi.net/bible/mat_12_34

Printed in the United States
127616LV00003B/3/P